Citizens of the World

Citizens of the World

*Political Engagement and Policy
Attitudes of Millennials across the Globe*

STELLA M. ROUSE
JARED McDONALD
RICHARD N. ENGSTROM
MICHAEL J. HANMER
ROBERTO GONZÁLEZ
SIUGMIN LAY
DANIEL MIRANDA

Oxford University Press is a department of the University of Oxford. It furthers
the University's objective of excellence in research, scholarship, and education
by publishing worldwide. Oxford is a registered trade mark of Oxford University
Press in the UK and certain other countries.

Published in the United States of America by Oxford University Press
198 Madison Avenue, New York, NY 10016, United States of America.

© Oxford University Press 2023

All rights reserved. No part of this publication may be reproduced, stored in
a retrieval system, or transmitted, in any form or by any means, without the
prior permission in writing of Oxford University Press, or as expressly permitted
by law, by license, or under terms agreed with the appropriate reproduction
rights organization. Inquiries concerning reproduction outside the scope of the
above should be sent to the Rights Department, Oxford University Press, at the
address above.

You must not circulate this work in any other form
and you must impose this same condition on any acquirer.

Library of Congress Control Number: 2022029522
ISBN 978-0-19-759938-9 (pbk.)
ISBN 978-0-19-759937-2 (hbk.)

DOI: 10.1093/oso/9780197599372.001.0001

Contents

1. Introduction—U21 Global Survey: Millennials as Citizens of the World   1

2. Millennials and the Shift toward a Global Identity   11

3. Millennials as Digital Natives: News Consumption and Political Preferences   39

4. How (Politically) Conventional Are Millennials? Exploring Preferences for Varying Forms of Political Participation   64

5. Duty-Based Citizenship, Engaged Citizenship, or Somewhere in the Middle? Millennials' Interest in Serving the Public   89

6. Millennials: The Global Perspective and the Future of a Shared Generational Identity   101

Global Millennial Survey Questionnaire   119
Notes   129
Works Cited   131
Index   147

1

Introduction—U21 Global Survey

Millennials as Citizens of the World

The COVID-19 pandemic and protests against police brutality have highlighted both the unique hardships the Millennial Generation continues to face as well as its prominence in a burgeoning international movement for social justice. Both of these events underscore a cultural generation gap that is rooted in such factors as diversity, formative events, and technological developments (among others). Why is it important to study the Millennial Generation? What are this generation's political, social, and economic attitudes, and how will these attitudes, compared to those of older adults, influence democratic governance around the world?

Today the Millennial Generation, the age cohort born between the early 1980s and the late 1990s, is the most educated, digitally connected, and globalized in the history of the world. In a number of countries, Millennials are the largest generational cohort. In the United States, the Millennial generation exceeds one-quarter of the population and is the most diverse in American history (Frey 2018; Rouse and Ross 2018). Around the world, the Millennial Generation encompasses 1.8 billion people (a quarter of the world's population) and will soon produce a majority of the political, economic, and social leaders.

It is thus not surprising that social commentators, concerned about how society is changing and how it will continue to change, have placed an emphasis on understanding the Millennial Generation. This cohort generally does not remember the pre-internet world and has had access to computerized communication

Citizens of the World. Stella M. Rouse, Jared McDonald, Richard N. Engstrom, Michael J. Hanmer, Roberto González, Siugmin Lay, and Daniel Miranda, Oxford University Press. © Oxford University Press 2023. DOI: 10.1093/oso/9780197599372.003.0001

2 CITIZENS OF THE WORLD

systems and communities for virtually their entire lives. Social critics wonder how this group of potential leaders and decision-makers will integrate into institutions created by generations accustomed to very different forms of interactions: institutions that move more slowly, function under the assumption that individuals have less access to immediate information, and delegate decision-making and action to others who are expected to negotiate the details.

Generational theorists have found that generational cohorts can form a "core persona" based on their shared experiences and interests (Howe and Strauss 2000; Pew Research Center 2014; Rouse and Ross 2018) and that the issue priorities and policy preferences that emerge from this persona can create the conditions for social change. Braungart and Braungart (1986) argue that a "political generation," one that mobilizes to implement change based on their shared preferences, has the potential to align institutions and policies to their values.

Of course, not all generations have equal interests or experiences. The Silent Generation, those born between the Great Depression and the start of World War II, was famously interested in pragmatic solutions and "working within the system," as opposed to leading social change (Howe 2014). It is also the case that a "generational frame" can describe only a generational cohort's central tendencies, as not all members of the generation conform to the group's worldview. Whether the Millennial Generation makes its mark as an agent of lasting political and social change depends a great deal on the extent to which there is a common core of values and preferences, how widely those preferences are shared, and members' collective interest in participating in public life to a degree that will influence future institutions and policies.

In this book, we argue that Millennials indeed share a core persona. Millennials grew up experiencing the terrorist attacks of September 11 and the subsequent and yet to be interrupted "war on terror." The global proliferation of the internet and smartphones and the increased interconnectedness of countries around the world also occurred largely during their formative years. In many countries, early adulthood for many Millennials was marked by rates of unemployment and underemployment that surpass those of their parents and grandparents, making them the first generation in the modern era to have higher rates of poverty than their predecessors at the same age. The recession resulting from the global COVID-19 pandemic has further punctuated the economic instability of Millennials, at a time when many in this generation are entering their prime working years (Van Dam 2020). The Millennial Generation will increasingly be in leadership positions during an era of rapid change and uncertainty, shaped by factors such as the global pandemic, economic hardship, demands for racial justice, and the retrenchment of the United States from the global stage. Simply put, making sense of what is to come requires a deeper understanding of what defines the Millennial Generation's persona, their attachment to various identities, how they perceive the need for change, and the tools they will use for enacting that change.

This book explores the political attitudes and behaviors of Millennials relative to older adults across eight countries: Australia, Chile, Mexico, New Zealand, South Africa, South Korea, the United Kingdom, and the United States. This list is by no means exhaustive, but it is diverse in a number of ways, allowing us to identify the extent to which attitudes and behaviors are common across borders formed by land and sea. We anchor our discussion in politics, but our intent is to speak to a broad range of issues that motivate scholars across disciplines to investigate further. Our focus is on a traditional versus an emerging global identity and how news consumption shapes political attitudes, civic engagement, public service motivation, and the general belief in one's ability to bring about political change. We find that Millennials are unique in a variety of ways, with important implications for domestic and international politics.

What Do We Know about Millennials?

Reports have given accounts of how Millennials are significantly slower to marry (Pew Research Center 2010), are less likely to say that two-parent families are important (Pew Research Center 2010), and are more likely to delay purchasing a home (Urban Institute 2018). These trends may indicate a change in how Millennials relate to social institutions and cultural benchmarks. They may also be an artifact of the more challenging economic environment that Millennials encountered when entering the workforce. Fewer high-paying jobs, recent economic downturns, student debt, and rising housing costs likely factor into the decision not to take on long-term responsibilities and expenses regardless of any attitudinal change. Yet the economic environment in which Millennials were socialized may have itself caused long-term attitudinal change, differentiating Millennials from older age cohorts. In line with research on Millennials in the United States, we show that the tumultuous times in which Millennials around the world have grown up and entered adulthood have indeed shaped the ways in which they view politics and society.

Millennials were born during the longest period of economic growth in the twentieth century but entered the job market in the worst recession since the 1930s (Thompson 2012; Rouse and Ross 2018). According to the Pew Research Center (2014), Millennials are the first generation in the modern era to experience greater poverty and unemployment than the two preceding generations. They have the highest education levels of any previous generation, and also carry a relatively large amount of student debt, which they have trouble paying back due to the economic climate when they joined the job market (Ferri-Reed 2013). The experience of graduating into recessions and tight job markets with relatively high loads of debt is shared among many Millennials and likely influences how they make life choices that are different from those made by older generations.

The Millennial identity also likely affects this cohort's views about jobs and employment. For example, Millennials are frequently reported to be less loyal employees and are comfortable with the idea that they will change jobs often over the course of their lives (Akumina 2019). A Gallup (2017) report found that Millennial employees were more interested in being mentored and finding meaning in their work than in hitting performance metrics. Retaining Millennial employees, Gallup suggests, requires that managers work to find ways to engage them and communicate the benefits of remaining at the company in terms of their individual goals. The loyal "company" man or woman is another institution Millennials seem to be leaving behind. Whether and how attitudes about institutions vary around the world can help us better understand this cohort's relationship with other social and political structures.

Implications for Democracy and Governance

Why should we care about Millennials? One overarching reason is that they are the largest generation of adults both in the United States and around the world,[1] and this fact comes with political implications. Not only are they the largest voting bloc, but they are gradually entering the period of their lives when they would traditionally assume society's political and community leadership roles. Understanding to what extent and how they are interested in engaging in political life has profound implications for how the first half of the twenty-first century will be governed. How do they see the world? What problems are important? How should those problems be addressed?

This raises another important question: To what extent are Millennial attitudes the product of country-specific conditions, and to what extent are they more universal? If a Millennial mindset exists across national boundaries, this has implications not only

6 CITIZENS OF THE WORLD

for the political prospects of certain policies and candidates in the near future, but for democracy globally. What will democracy look like in twenty or thirty years? The Millennial Generation will have a lot to say about that, and it makes sense to investigate how their preferences may influence the way democracies work (and how well they work) in the long term.

What Don't We Know about Millennials?

The idea that Millennials are a global political generation is intriguing, but finding out if it is a reality requires an international study establishing to what extent Millennials in different parts of the world share values and policy preferences, and to what extent they are in agreement about acting on those preferences. Several studies have found that Millennials are more likely to "think globally" (Zogby and Kuhl 2013; Rouse and Ross 2018), but this is not to say that they have the potential to be a global political force or actually have commonalities that truly make them global citizens.

To address these questions we worked with a team of researchers who fielded public opinion surveys exploring questions about policy preferences, attitudes about political and social divisions, political engagement, and approaches to problem solving in eight democracies around the world. In each country, data were gathered from approximately six hundred respondents, half of whom were members of the Millennial Generation and half of whom were older adults. This allows us to compare the responses of Millennials to those of older respondents. Over three thousand online surveys were completed by the residents of the eight countries, representing various ages, incomes, religions, education levels, and other important characteristics. By analyzing those responses both within each country and across national boundaries, we are able to shed light on how Millennial attitudes on governance and policy differ from those of previous generations. We are also able to examine the extent to which those preferences are country-specific or are shared globally.

The Arab Spring, a series of antigovernment protests that occurred in the Middle East during the early 2010s, was largely seen as a movement spearheaded by Millennials (Cole 2014). Much of the movement's success was due to Millennials' savvy use of social media, which facilitated the organizing of activists and informing the outside world about real-time developments (Pew Research Center 2012). These protests are great examples of how Millennials from different countries coordinated an uprising as a result of a number of common characteristics, such as being highly educated, having a sense of cosmopolitanism, and leveraging technology (Cole 2014). As we will discuss throughout the book, these, among a number of shared characteristics and experiences, come together to form what is known as the Millennial Generation identity or persona that provides a theoretical baseline for understanding the attitudes and opinions of this cohort (Rouse and Ross 2018).

Utilizing the Millennial Generation identity, this study will explore the similarity and differences of Millennials in various political, social, and economic environments around the world. It will allow for intergenerational comparison, as well as comparisons to older cohorts. As previous scholars have noted (Erkulwater 2016; Rouse and Ross 2018), there is a distinction between lifecycle and generational (cohort) effects. The former refers to changes that occur as individuals age; these changes are sequential and are fairly universal (Braungart and Braungart 1986). The latter is based on the shared social and historical experiences of those born during the same era (Erkulwater 2016). When considering political, social, and economic attitudes, both lifecycle and generational effects are involved, and the two are not always easy to disentangle. Further complicating the narrative is that age plays an important role in the evaluation of both lifecycle and generational effects, as it helps shape the way events are experienced by a group (Rouse and Ross 2018). Young and old people react in different ways to the same

8 CITIZENS OF THE WORLD

event, depending upon their generational characteristics as well as their current stage of life (Riley 1973). Once again, we can point to the different expectations for how COVID-19 affects generations (both in the short and long term), as well as how it influences people at varying stages of their life.

In this book, we are interested in understanding and comparing how divergent generational attitudes about political, social, and economic norms affect issues of governance in different countries around the world. This chapter has introduced the theory of the Millennial Generation identity. We outline the importance of this identity and why Millennials around the world will be front and center in the future direction of democratic countries and the evolution of a global community.

Chapter 2 provides an overview of our survey results, highlighting how Millennials distinguish themselves as global rather than national citizens, and pointing out which countries do and do not conform to particular global trends. We find strong evidence that Millennials do, indeed, feel more comfortable than older generations expressing a global identity, as opposed to more traditionally local identities. Still, we show that national identities continue to be strong across all countries and all age groups, while identities related to race, religion, gender, and class are especially important for small subgroups of respondents.

Chapter 3 looks at the implications that generational differences in media usage have for governance as traditional media outlets are marginalized in favor of more personalized options such as smartphones, the internet, and social media. Broadly, we find that Millennials disproportionately rely on new media (e.g., the internet and social media) for political information. Although these news sources are prone to disinformation, we do not find evidence that Millennials have a more difficult time differentiating accurate information from misinformation. We further find trends to suggest that the Millennial reliance on online news sources leads them adopt attitudes that transcend international borders. In other words, older generations differ greatly in their political attitudes from one country to another, while Millennials exhibit greater consistency from a global perspective.

Chapter 4 evaluates how political efficacy differs between Millennial and non-Millennial respondents. The findings indicate that Millennials are no more disillusioned with politics than non-Millennials, yet the ways they prefer to engage in politics differ greatly from more traditional, duty-based forms of engagement such as voting. Millennials attribute less importance to voting than do non-Millennials but report equal or higher rates of participation in participating in demonstrations, making political donations, and engaging in online discussions about important political topics. We draw implications for how those differences may change how people connect with political and social issues.

Chapter 5 builds on the findings of Chapter 4, asking how the changing environment uncovered in the surveys will affect how the next generation of leaders see public service, most especially at the level of local politics, and what it will take to engage them in tackling public service challenges. Consistent with the findings throughout the book, we show that although Millennials report voting less frequently in local elections, they are generally more willing to engage in local political activities and report feeling a strong sense of efficacy about their ability to perform public service jobs. These findings provide some comfort that, despite reports of Millennials feeling alienated from their communities, there are reasons for optimism that they will engage in the work necessary to perform leadership duties in local government and society more generally.

Finally, Chapter 6 assesses the book's findings as a whole, and draws conclusions about what we can expect from the generation of "global citizens" our analyses have uncovered. In each of these chapters, we rely on research across several fields, including political science, psychology, and public policy in order to better understand the implications of an emerging generation with different experiences and perspectives about their political and social outlooks. We hope our findings will draw interest from international scholars to include generation as a key measure for assessing how group identities influence attitudes about governance and civic engagement.

Previous studies have suggested that Millennials are optimistic about a better future for the world and that they are willing to embrace the challenge of bringing about change (Rouse and Ross 2018). Are they positioned to be a political force that makes that happen? We find that Millennials do share many values across countries and that they are positioned to use the communication, information, and collaborative tools, relatively unique to their adult generation, to be effective public leaders in a manner that is different from other generations.

2

Millennials and the Shift toward a Global Identity

> [My community is] multi-faith, multi-cultural. Interesting place filled with life and joy.
> —Twenty-one-year-old from the United Kingdom

> My community has no help for poor people. My community has no help for medical care for single white American-born citizens.
> —Fifty-six-year-old from the United States

Millennials, whom we define as those born between 1983 and 2000,[1] grew up at a time of great change both in the individual nations we survey and globally. Millennials experienced the terrorist attacks of September 11 and the ensuing "war on terror." They were the first generation to grow up with widespread availability of the internet and entered the workforce at roughly the same time as the Great Recession of 2008. In short, they came of age during a time of transition. They also came of age in an era in which the countries we examine were undergoing major economic and demographic changes. These changes have come with growing pains, as new divisions within society emerged to replace the old, and old and young alike faced uncertain futures. Yet unlike previous generations, the career prospects of Millennials are uniquely grim. Most experts agree that the Millennial generation will be the first to

Citizens of the World. Stella M. Rouse, Jared McDonald, Richard N. Engstrom, Michael J. Hanmer, Roberto González, Siugmin Lay, and Daniel Miranda, Oxford University Press. © Oxford University Press 2023. DOI: 10.1093/oso/9780197599372.003.0002

12 CITIZENS OF THE WORLD

earn less than their parents over the course of their lifetime (World Economic Forum 2016).

In this chapter, we look at how the core identities that define Millennials are different from those that define older adults. We do so by examining a diverse group of countries: Australia, Chile, Mexico, New Zealand, South Africa, South Korea, the United Kingdom, and the United States. We find that Millennial citizens bring a global perspective to the way they view themselves and their political environment. We suggest that this perspective is largely attributable to their Millennial identity or persona—a unique set of values, circumstances, and experiences that comprise the formative characteristics of this generation. This identity is largely grounded in cultural shifts occurring from social, economic, and political events that took place during the time in which the Millennial generation came of age (Rouse and Ross 2018).

While the time period critical for Millennial socialization was characterized by the rise of global terrorism, armed conflicts in various parts of the world, and economic insecurity, it was also marked by an increased sense of global interconnectedness. In the post–Cold War society, globalization and advances in technology created the widespread availability of the internet, social media, and smartphones, allowing for the free flow of information and a greater sense of global community. This globalization also brought with it important demographic changes in the countries we examine here. Foreign-born individuals in 2015 made up 28% of the population of Australia (compared to 20% in 1980), 15% of the population of the United States (compared to 6.2% in 1980), and 13% of the population of the United Kingdom (compared to 6.2% in 1980) (United Nations 2017; Pison 2019).

With the analyses presented here, we examine how Millennials and non-Millennials view themselves and the world they occupy. Questions surrounding citizens' salient identities have long been of interest to scholars around the world, as these identities influence citizens' attitudes and behaviors, from vote choice and turnout to the capacity to care for and empathize with others. These identities also serve to inform citizens about which people are "deserving" of government aid, thereby influencing the way responsive governments distribute resources and address issues of social justice.

Social change in many of the countries we examine affects citizens differently depending on the generation to which they belong. What we find is that individuals of all ages remain deeply identified with their national identities. Overwhelmingly, national identity is the most salient individual characteristic across countries and age groups. Yet Millennials are far more likely than older generations to identify as a "citizen of the world," an attitude known as *cosmopolitanism*, "being a citizen of a larger global community" (Nussbaum 1996). Like the twenty-one-year-old quoted in the chapter epigraph, Millennials have come of age in a much smaller and closer world than the one experienced by older generations. They know little of a society that does not include the free flow of information, services, goods, and people across both real and virtual borders. Given the characteristics of the world in which they have come of age, they embrace multiculturalism and a cosmopolitan identity. They see an advantage to rejecting older, more exclusive labels and moving toward a universal sense of human identity. This interconnectedness affords opportunities to develop empathy for and understanding of different cultures. It allows those who embrace cosmopolitanism to take in different viewpoints to inform their attitudes and opinions, and thus allows for the examination of issues from a global perspective (Vertovec and Cohen 2002; Hopper 2007; Rouse and Ross 2018). Older citizens, like the fifty-six-year-old American quoted in the other epigraph, generally tend to not see growing cosmopolitanism as a positive trend. They tend to view governmental priorities as shifting away from native-born citizens and toward outsider groups they view as less deserving (see, e.g., Van Oorschot 2006). This shift away from nationalism and toward a more cosmopolitan sense of community is likely to

14   CITIZENS OF THE WORLD

have far-reaching implications for global politics in years to come. We begin to explore these differences with the analyses presented in this chapter.

The rest of the chapter follows in three sections. We first discuss the importance of political socialization during childhood and adolescence for lifelong political attitudes and behavior. We then turn to the ways in which salient identities, often those we develop early in life, form a perceptual screen through which we view social and political events. Finally, we turn to a discussion of our data and results.

When we ask Millennials and non-Millennials to rate themselves on a scale from 1 to 10 on a host of identities, we find that Millennials are far more likely to eschew labels. While many non-Millennials claim the strongest sense of identity (10 on the scale) across a host of differing characteristics, Millennials are generally less willing to do this. National identity is the strongest for most citizens across the globe regardless of age, yet even here a notable gap exists between Millennials and non-Millennials. One of the few exceptions, however, is when it comes to the label "citizen of the world." This more inclusive label is more likely to be claimed by Millennials than by previous generations. We additionally consider whether Millennials feel a sense of kinship with other Millennials, generating a shared identity. We find varying levels of a shared generational identity across the countries we examine. We also find that generational identity matters more in some countries than others, making it easier for Millennials to organize in countries where generational identity is highly salient than where it is not. We then turn to a discussion of religious identity among Millennials and non-Millennials. More than any of the other identities we examine, religion is the one in which the specifics of each country matter most. In countries like South Africa and the United States, it is one of the most salient identities for citizens, while in many of the other countries we survey, it fails to register for most people. Last, we consider matters of race, ethnicity, gender, and class. While these identities are overall less salient for both Millennials and non-Millennials, we note important differences that persist across ages that may be meaningful in the way citizens approach the political world.

The Political Socialization of Millennials

Scholars studying the causes of political identity emphasize the importance of early life (i.e., childhood and adolescence) experiences. Political attitudes, identity, and engagement are formed early in life and help predict lifelong political behavior across a host of activities, such as voting, contacting elected officials, volunteering, and participating in political demonstrations (Easton and Dennis 1969; Jennings and Niemi 1981; Niemi and Sobieszek 1977). While a number of studies in political science and sociology find that there is some level of "plasticity," whereby major events alter political attitudes and behavior (Alwin and Krosnick 1991), experiences obtained during childhood and adolescence still have important predictive power on attitudes and behavior much later in life (Kinder and Sears 1985). The scholarly consensus is that, while some postadolescence change can occur (a lifecycle effect), many of our most important political identities, such as partisanship and ideology, are developed early in life and are often shared by those who became politically conscious at the same time (a cohort effect) (Braungart and Braungart 1986).

What factors shape individuals during these impressionable years? Many of the factors scholars associate with political socialization work at a micro level; these will differ based on the unique attributes of the communities to which young citizens belong. These factors are varied, but include the effect of parents, teachers, religious institutions, civic organizations, and the broader community in which children are raised and socialized. Parents are perhaps the single most important influence on the political socialization of young citizens. Parents raise their children's level of awareness in politics when they themselves are politically involved (Beck and Jennings 1982; Jennings and Niemi 1968), and their income level helps determine their children's level of education and socioeconomic status (Verba, Schlozman, and Burns 2005). Schools likewise exert a great deal of influence on political and social attitudes (Hello et al. 2004). Although schools are a partial proxy for socioeconomic status (Campbell 2009; Nie, Junn, and Stehlik-Barry 1996), they also have an independent effect on the identities and attitudes of pupils; namely, schools have an important effect on political engagement and attitudes when these values are not provided by the parents (Neundorf, Niemi, and Smets 2016).

Despite the importance of micro factors, macro factors similarly shape individual political preferences and behavior. These factors apply to all members of the same generation, regardless of the circumstances of family or community. More important for the purposes of the present research, these factors can create a uniform sense of political identity for each generation. The Millennial Generation identity, in particular, includes such factors as increasing demographic diversity in many countries, social and economic globalization, and the proliferation of technology (Rouse and Ross 2018). Due in large part to these factors, we posit that peer networks are one way Millennials develop a common political identity. This runs counter to the traditional scholarly view of social networks' role in political socialization (Langton 1967). Social networks, in many ways, are dependent on the community in which one is raised and may therefore be considered a micro-level influence on political attitudes. Undoubtedly, the networks young people develop in schools and in their communities influence the ways in which they view the political world and vary greatly depending on the affluence, diversity, and interconnectedness of the cities and towns in which they live. Yet contemporary networks are no longer bound by those individuals we meet in school. Social media is now a powerful influence in transmitting a shared sense of community and culture within a peer group (Wattenberg 2008).

Social media provides a cue for Millennials about the norms and expectations that exist for young people relative to other age groups. And unlike previous generations, Millennials spend vastly more time on the internet and social media. A 2018 study by Global Web Index estimated that Millennials spend more than two and a half hours on social media a day compared to the less than one hour and fifteen minutes spent on social media by Baby Boomers.[2]

In recent years, Facebook, Twitter, and Instagram have been used as organizing tools for young citizens to express their dissatisfaction with government and society. Moreover, Millennials who use social media as an organizing tool often make their generational identity an explicit motivator for political action. In Hong Kong, young pro-democracy demonstrators used social media as an organizing tool for popular rallies and to influence public opinion. Protesters circulating images of police brutality on Facebook and Instagram brought international attention to the issue, helping to bring widespread condemnation on the Chinese government for its role in the violence (CNBC 2019). Social media has served a pivotal role for other protest movements as well, such as Occupy Wall Street, the "Stop Kony" campaign, and revolutionary movements during the Arab Spring, yet it has also played a role in conveying generational norms outside of explicit political protests. For example, the "OK Boomer" retort, which became popular among Gen-Zers and Millennials on social media in 2019, exemplified a shared resentment among younger individuals toward their forebears and signaled a desired shift in power away from the Baby Boomers toward younger groups (*Vox* 2019).

Beyond peer effects, major political events play an important role in the political socialization of citizens during their impressionable years. These events further generate a common set of identities and values among members of the same generation (Sapiro 2004). Bartels and Jackman (2014) find that adolescents are highly sensitive to national and world political events, which can shape subsequent attitudes. While the Vietnam War and the Watergate

18 CITIZENS OF THE WORLD

break-in are viewed as the two watershed moments that shaped the attitudes of the Baby Boom generation (Dinas 2013; Erikson and Stoker 2011), Millennials grew up in the shadows of 9/11 and the war on terror (Rouse and Ross 2018).

In addition to the important political events shaping Millennial attitudes, the political role models for Millennials look very different from those of prior generations and reflect a greater sense of diversity and interrelatedness in the global community. From Barack Obama and Malala Yousafzai, to more recent figures such as antigun activist X González and environmental activist Greta Thunberg, the people at the forefront of global and domestic politics are often younger, racially diverse, and increasingly female. Scholars often find that a more varied set of role models can increase political participation and a sense of political consciousness (Atkeson 2003; Campbell and Wolbrecht 2006; Fox and Lawless 2014). We find that Millennials' attitudes and identities differ strongly from previous generations, suggesting that the unique events and role models they experienced profoundly shaped their worldview. While there is a general disaffection toward politics among Millennials (which we discuss in later chapters), there is also less pride in identifying strongly as a citizen of one's country and a stronger tendency to reject restrictive labels, opting instead for the broader "citizen of the world" moniker.

The Importance of Identity

With the Global Millennial Survey (GMS), we look at how Millennials and non-Millennials across the world view themselves. We do so with an eye toward how these identities shape policy attitudes and a willingness to engage the political system, at both global and national levels. We pay particular attention to how the identities of Millennials, the largest cohort in the world, affects these perspectives. Scholars working in social and cognitive psychology argue that important social identities inform our political beliefs and influence the way citizens view the world. Social identity is defined as a "subjective sense of belonging" to a group (Tajfel 1981), and scholars maintain that this sense of belonging requires that individuals feel this attachment not only with a specific label (e.g., "Latino" or "Episcopalian") but with the group of people who similarly share the identity (e.g., Latinos and Episcopalians). Members of the group who rank high on measures of social identity tend to be more motivated to spend time with others who belong to that group and to promote the welfare of the group as a whole. They are also more likely to differentiate between members of the in-group and members of the out-group, which can increase hostility and resentment felt by members of one group toward members of another. Members of each group are thought to derive individual self-esteem from the esteem of the group as a whole (Crocker and Major 1989; Tajfel and Turner 1979).

Identities become more salient when they are under threat. Jardina (2019) notes that identity politics has historically been viewed through the identities of racial and ethnic minorities. The status of racial minorities in the social hierarchy made those identities particularly salient, while members of socially dominant groups exhibited weaker levels of identification. In the United States, Jardina finds that white citizens rarely felt a strong sense of belonging to the white community, as their unassailable position atop the social hierarchy meant that other divisions along religious or class lines would be more prominent. Recent shifts in demographics in many Western democracies, primarily through immigration, have made even the identity of historically dominant groups salient. Concern over a potential reorganizing of the social hierarchy generates a sense of threat, which primes the importance of white identity. For example, Jardina reports that more than 40% of white people in the United States rank high on measures of white identity, which has important implications for the types of policies they support, as well as their support for Donald Trump, whose electoral victory in 2016 was a shock to most (Sides, Tesler, and Vavreck 2018).

Examining identity in a global setting is a difficult task in that the important social cleavages that should make particular identities salient vary from country to country. Yet we made understanding identity a key component of the GMS. To do so, we asked respondents across all eight countries to estimate, on a scale from 1 to 10, how much they identified with eight different identities: citizens of their country (national identity), citizens of the world (cosmopolitan identity), members of their race (racial identity), religion (religious identity), ethnicity (ethnic identity), generation (generational identity), gender (gender identity), and class (class identity). We then asked them to select the single identity that was most important to them.

We find a Millennial generation that largely shies away from labels that serve to divide the population. Excluding the label "citizen of the world," we find that non-Millennials identify more strongly with a host of different identities. National identity is especially strong across all countries, though "citizen of the world" remains more popular among Millennials. In terms of other identities, we find limited evidence that Millennials feel a connection with those of their generation and that generational differences along religion, race, class, and gender depend greatly on the country under examination.

Millennials More Likely to Eschew Labels

Before proceeding to the responses of Millennials and non-Millennials across each of the individual identities, we consider the nature of labels in general for the different generations. We demonstrate in the next section that Millennials are more positive toward the "citizen of the world" label than non-Millennials, yet the differences when looking at the ratings from 1 to 10 are often modest. Looking at the average rating for the seven other identities across all the countries in our survey—national identity, racial identity, religious identity, ethnic identity, generational identity, gender identity, and class identity (shown in Figure 2.1)—helps explain why. Older generations across most of the globe are more willing to accept labels that divide the in-group from the out-group. Only in Mexico do we see Millennials identify more strongly on average with these types of labels, and even here the differences are small.

In contrast, larger differences emerge when looking at Australia, Chile, South Korea, and the United States. In all of these countries, the differences between Millennials and non-Millennials are greater than a third of a point. (In Chile and South Korea the differences are nearly a full half point.) When we interpret responses to these scales, we have to grade respondents in relative rather than absolute terms. There are situations in which the differences between Millennials and non-Millennials on the 1–10 scale are modest, yet much more meaningful differences emerge when we look at the single most important identity. In some cases,

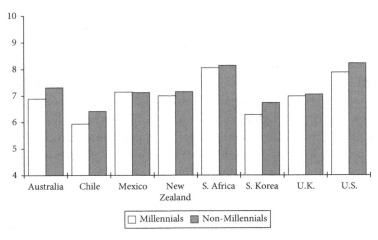

Figure 2.1 Mean Identity Rating on Seven of Eight Identities (1–10 Scale, excludes "Citizen of the World")

22 CITIZENS OF THE WORLD

Millennials rate themselves lower on the scale, yet more of them select those identities as the single most important ones. This, in part, may come down to the fact that Millennials feel a subjectively weaker attachment across the board to identities that serve to divide society. This less exclusive outlook, we argue, has important implications for the type of society we should expect as Millennials grow in political and economic power.

National Identity Matters, but Millennials Increasingly Value Their Cosmopolitan Identity

We next present the full results for the GMS on questions related to identity. Unlike in Figure 2.1, where we aggregate seven of the eight identities, the graphs shown in Figures 2.2a and 2.2b present the average responses in each country for each identity, broken out by age group. Figures 2.3a and 2.3b present the percentage of respondents in each country and age group that selected that identity as the single most important one.

A number of important trends are apparent in these graphs, but perhaps the clearest is the degree to which people across the globe identify as citizens of their country. Across all countries and all age groups, the average response was no less than a 7 on the 1–10 scale. Nationalism appears especially strong in the United States and South Africa, though it is relatively less salient in South Korea and Chile. In the United States, 74% of all respondents rated their national citizenship a 10, the highest rating, while in South Korea only 34% of respondents chose similarly.

More important, however, is the gap we see in strength of national identity between Millennials and older citizens. With the notable exception of South Africa, Millennials are less strongly identified with their country compared to older generations. These gaps are especially pronounced in Australia, Chile, New Zealand,

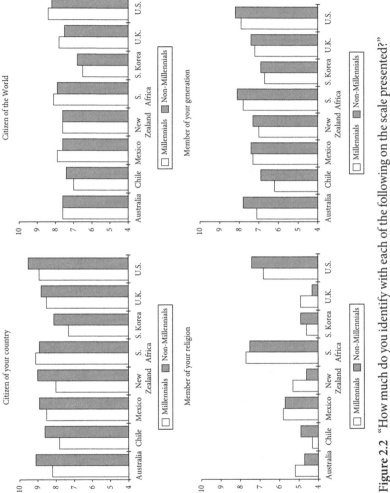

Figure 2.2 "How much do you identify with each of the following on the scale presented?" (1–10 Scale, Mean Rating)

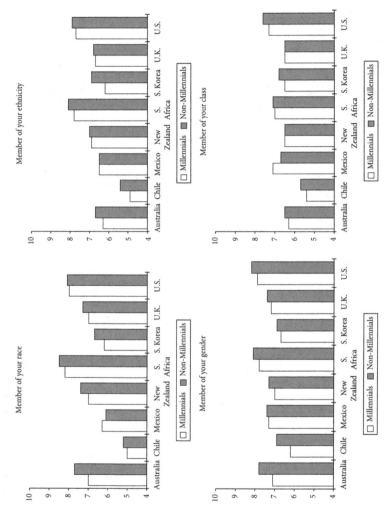

Figure 2.2 Continued.

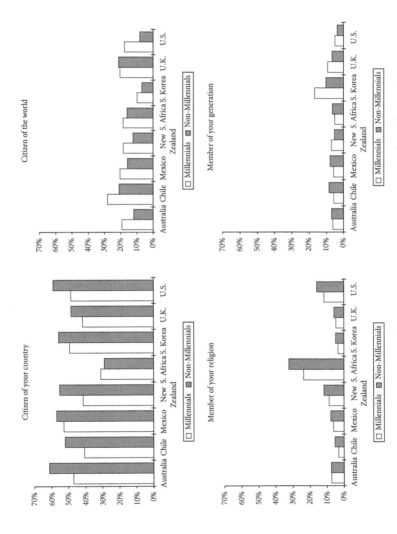

Figure 2.3 "Which one of these identities is most important to you today? Please select one.

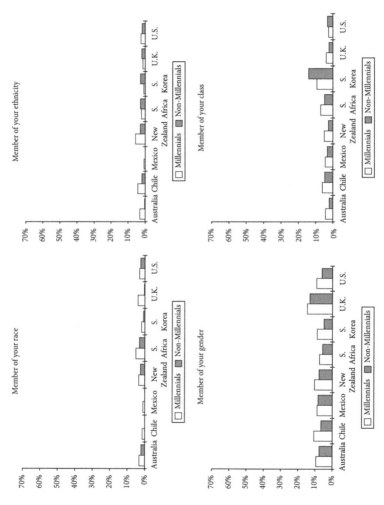

Figure 2.3 Continued.

South Korea, and the United States, where the gaps are all greater than half a point. To put these gaps in perspective, take the example of Australia. On average, the gap between Millennials and non-Millennials was just under 1 point (8.2 vs. 9.1, respectively). This difference is driven largely by the proportion of respondents who chose the most extreme high value for national citizenship. Among those non-Millennials, 71% of Australians chose the highest value of 10. Only 5% of respondents in this group rated themselves at 5 or less, demonstrating a strong national identity among this group. Among Millennial Australians, however, only 48% rated themselves at 10 on national identity, and 11% rated themselves at 5 or lower. In absolute terms, both Millennials and non-Millennials are high in national identity, yet there Millennials are consistently less enthusiastic than their older compatriots about the national citizen identity.

While asking people to rate themselves on a 1–10 scale is informative, we also examine which identity Millennials and non-Millennials consider to be the most salient. Figures 2.3a and 2.3b show the results for the individual identities included on the GMS. When asked to select the single strongest identity, again we find that national identity is the overwhelming pick. More than 50% of those thirty-five and older picked "Citizen of your country" in six of the eight countries surveyed. Yet Millennials are far less likely to pick their national identity as the strongest one, with greater than 10-point gaps appearing in Australia, Chile, New Zealand, and the United States. South Africa stands out as unique, both in terms of lower levels of overall nationalism (roughly 30% across all respondents) and as the only country where Millennials showed a stronger sense of national identity compared to non-Millennials. In part, this is likely due to the majority of older South Africans' refusal to identify with the apartheid-era regime. Younger South Africans have been raised in a country in which they are afforded the basic rights of citizenship. As we explore later in this chapter, we also believe the unique results for South Africa can be attributed to

28 CITIZENS OF THE WORLD

the importance of religious identity for all citizens and its outsized importance among non-Millennials.

When we compare the ratings on "Citizen of your country" with those offered for "Citizen of the world," we get a better picture for the different ways Millennials view themselves. While a sense of cosmopolitan citizenship has not surpassed national citizenship among Millennials, they largely rate themselves as feeling more closely identified as citizens of the world than do older generations. In the United States, 48% of Millennials rated themselves at 10 on "Citizen of the world." This rating is admittedly lower than the 65% who rated themselves at the maximum on "Citizen of the United States." Yet the gap among American Millennials pales in comparison to the gap among older age groups. Among non-Millennials, 47% rated themselves at 10 on "Citizen of the world," while 82% did so on "Citizen of the United States."

This trend continues when we look at the survey item asking citizens to select their most important identity. Millennials were more likely to select "Citizen of the world" in seven of the eight countries surveyed. Differences were especially pronounced in Australia, Chile, New Zealand, and the United States. While national identity remains the strongest identity, even among the more cosmopolitan Millennial generation, there is strong evidence of a shift in perspective that makes this cohort more open to culturally diverse viewpoints.

What should we make of this shift among Millennials away from their national identity and toward a more cosmopolitan sense of citizenship relative to previous generations? Research in the American context finds that younger generations are more diverse, better educated, and digitally connected (Rouse and Ross 2018; Pew Research Center 2018), making contact with individuals of different nationalities more likely. We find here that the shift toward a more global worldview is not specific to any one country but reflects a broader shift among younger generations away from accepting restrictive labels. Across most of the identities included

MILLENNIALS AND SHIFT TOWARD A GLOBAL IDENTITY   29

on the GMS, older citizens claimed to feel a stronger sense of attachment than did Millennials. Yet on the relatively less restrictive or divisive "Citizen of the world" label, Millennials by and large claimed stronger levels of attachment. This more universal approach to identity, and the rejection of in-group/out-group divisions that follows, indicates a greater ability to empathize with groups that are different from one's own.

Is There a Millennial Identity?

In addition to examining the types of identities that Millennials and non-Millennials consider most central to their concept of self, we examine whether there is a sense of group consciousness Millennials have with others in their generation. Do Millennials feel a greater sense of kinship with fellow Millennials relative to people from other generations? The evidence we present here is mixed. When asked to rate their level of attachment to their generational identity, Millennials in all eight countries offer lower levels of generational identity than those in older age groups. Yet, as we noted previously, Millennials are less likely to accept labels generally; that is, they have a tendency toward individualism or universalism and away from labels that might exclude others, which might limit the degree to which they will claim to identify strongly with the "Millennial" label.

When we force respondents to choose the one identity that is most important to them, Millennials exhibit a greater degree of generational identity. In New Zealand, South Korea, the United Kingdom, and the United States, a greater percentage of Millennials compared to older groups chose their generational identity as the single most important identity.

South Korea stands out in particular because it is the only country where generational identity was selected by more than 10% of respondents. It is also where the gap between Millennials and non-Millennials is the largest. While we can only speculate as to why South Korea is unique, it may be because it is one of the countries where Millennials' earning prospects relative to past generations is most disadvantaged. Millennial unemployment remains far higher than that of older generations, and wages have stagnated while property values have skyrocketed (Reuters 2019). A recent study from the Pew Research Center (2014a) found that Millennials are generally pessimistic about the direction of their country and feel that they will have fewer opportunities to succeed than did their parents. Our results suggest that disillusionment among South Korean Millennials over the direction of the country and their relationship with prior generations has made generational identity highly salient across the entire country, but especially among younger citizens.

South Korea, however, remains something of an outlier when it comes to generational identity. Looking at the number of people who selected generational identity as the single most important identity on the list, we find that generational identity consistently ranked behind national identity, cosmopolitan identity, and often gender and religious identities. It appears, then, that the differences in the way Millennials view themselves have more to do with a rejection of labels used by past generations and less to do with a common sense of purpose shared with those of the same cohort.

Religious Identity at the National and International Levels

Unlike identities surrounding national, cosmopolitan, and generational identity, we do not find consistent trends with religious identity among Millennials. In terms of subjective feelings of closeness with others of the same religion, the differences between Millennials and non-Millennials are modest. Millennials identify more strongly with their religion in five of the eight countries we examine, though none of the differences is much more than a half point. Moreover, those countries with the greatest differences between Millennials and older citizens, such as Chile, New Zealand, and the United Kingdom, are those where general levels of identification with religion are the lowest. Respondents in South Africa and the United States rate religious identity more strongly, with a more notable drop-off in religious identity in the United States: 40% of Americans thirty-five and older rated themselves at the maximum in terms of religious identity, compared to 31% of Millennials. While these differences are important, the country a respondent lives in appears to play a much bigger role in terms of religious identity than the generation to which a respondent belongs.

While Millennials claim roughly the same level of identification with their religious group as non-Millennials, we find a somewhat different story when we ask respondents to select the single most important identity. In all eight countries surveyed, a higher percentage of non-Millennials select their religious identity as the most important. Still, the differences are often modest, with only 1 or 2 percentage points separating Millennials and non-Millennials in Australia, Chile, Mexico, South Korea, and the United Kingdom. Furthermore, religious identity in these countries is the selection of less than 10% of the overall sample.

The biggest exception to this global trend is South Africa. Here, religious identity rivals even national identity in terms of overall salience: 30% of South African respondents selected their national identity as the most salient, compared to 28% who selected their religious identity. Among non-Millennials, religion outranks national identity as the single most important characteristic, with 32% of non-Millennials selecting religion compared to 29% selecting national identity. Among Millennials, only 24% selected religion, while a greater proportion, 31%, chose national identity. South Africa stands out among the countries we survey in that, rather than a shift away from national identity toward a cosmopolitan

32 CITIZENS OF THE WORLD

identity, Millennials appear to be moving away from their religious identity and toward a national identity.

That religion is a salient identity to citizens of South Africa is not a surprise. Citizens in less developed nations are generally more religious than those in highly developed countries (Norris and Inglehart 2004), and among the eight countries surveyed here, South Africa is significantly less developed than the others.[3]

Yet religious identity also has a unique and rich history in South Africa. While it has long held importance among both political elites and the masses, it played a particularly important role in the country during the apartheid era. The apartheid regime politicized religion, primarily through its association with the Dutch Reformed Church (Chipkin and Leatt 2011), though religion similarly held important political influence in the anti-apartheid movement, wherein leaders like Bishop Desmond Tutu employed a Christian sense of morality in the fight against the regime. Since the end of apartheid, South Africa has remained a deeply religious country, with more than 80% of South Africans claiming an affiliation with a Christian denomination (Pew Forum on Religion and Public Life 2009). Yet although religion was a key factor in organizing political movements during apartheid, it has played less of a role in recent decades as Millennials have been socialized and become politically active. Recent research finds that, although South Africans remain deeply religious, God is less important to them in how they view their day-to-day lives (Kotzé and Loubser 2017). This may be due to increasing levels of development and modernization that have occurred in the country over the past several decades. While it does not appear Millennials are any less religious than their older counterparts, religion is not as important to how they view themselves.

On matters of religion, then, we find a picture that does not fit a consistent narrative across generations and across countries. Overall, religion is less dominant than national or international identities. And though there is suggestive evidence that fewer

Millennials than non-Millennials view religion as the most important single factor in how they see themselves, we find that such a small percentage of our samples in each country picks religion as the most important identity that these differences tend to be modest. Still, in countries with a stronger history of religious tradition, such as South Africa and to a lesser extent the United States, religion continues to hold importance among a significant portion of society. In these places, its importance is driven primarily by older generations rather than Millennials.

Race, Ethnicity, Gender, and Class: The Paradox of Labels and Choice

Finally, we look at Millennials' sense of identity around race, ethnicity, gender, and class. We group these identities not because they are related in a theoretical sense but because they represent the tension between having citizens rate their subjective level of identity with a group and forcing them to choose the one that matters most to them. In some cases, we find that although the average respondent rates a given identity as highly important, exceedingly few respondents select that identity as the single most important one. Conversely, other identities are of relatively low importance, on average, and yet an important subset of respondents selects those identities as the most salient. We refer to these as "identity publics," as they represent a small group of society, but one that is especially likely to use a particular identity as a motivator for engaging in political action.

Race and ethnicity are two categories in which respondents, on average, claim a strong sense of identity but shy away from naming them as the most important. While a significant number of respondents rate themselves as strongly aligned with their racial group, in no country did more than 5% of respondents select race as the most important identity. For example, in New Zealand

34   CITIZENS OF THE WORLD

27% of respondents rated their racial identity at the maximum, yet only 3% selected race as the most salient. In the United States, the differences were even greater, with 46% rating their racial identity at 10 but only 3% selecting it as the most important identity.

These results also hold for matters of ethnicity, where respondents frequently claimed to feel a relatively strong sense of attachment but by and large shied away from claiming it was the single most important identity. Mexicans gave their ethnic identity an average rating of 6.5, with 22% rating it at 10. Yet when asked to pick only one identity that best described them, less than 1% selected ethnicity as the strongest identity.

With gender identity, a similar picture emerges. While both Millennials and non-Millennials show signs of strong gender identity, a relatively small percentage of respondents view gender as the most important among the alternatives provided. Furthermore, while non-Millennials claim to identify more strongly than Millennials with their gender in all eight countries surveyed, the trend is reversed when asked to name the most important identity.

With class identity, a similar paradox emerges whereby class appears to be a consistently stronger identity among non-Millennials, but is not selected as often to be the most important identity. In only one country (Mexico) did Millennials have a higher average rating on class-based identity, yet class identity was selected by more Millennials as the most important identity in six of the eight countries in our survey. An important exception to this is South Korea, where the relative racial and ethnic homogeneity leaves room for other identities to emerge as more salient.

How do we reconcile these somewhat contradictory findings? Considering the trends we find throughout the GMS, a number of important takeaways emerge. First, when we ask people to name the identity that is most important to them, we often miss out on the degree to which citizens still value the importance of other labels. Because so many respondents in all the countries we survey view themselves primarily as citizens of their country or citizens of the world, there are simply not many respondents left to drive the percentages for identities like race, gender, and class. Yet these identities still matter a great deal to individual citizens, even if they do not rise to the level of importance that national identity does. Prior scholarship finds that racial, gender-, and class-based divisions in society often inform perceptions of who qualifies as a true citizen of a country (Citrin, Reingold, and Green 1990). In other words, the fact that relatively few people choose their race as the most important category should not lead us to believe that racial identity isn't an important motivator of political behavior in many of the countries we examine.

Second, the findings here reconfirm what we pointed out previously: that Millennials are generally less willing to embrace labels. On a number of traits, but most especially race, Millennials on average rate themselves as less closely identified with a characteristic or trait. Yet when we probe further about which identities are most important, Millennials are more likely than their older counterparts to select traits like race or gender.

Finally, these results highlight the importance of small portions of the electorate who identify fiercely with particular identities. In political science, scholars often refer to "issue publics," or groups of people who are highly engaged in politics based on their interest in one particular area (Henderson 2014). Because issue publics pay a great deal of attention to political action in this one issue area, they can often achieve policy goals even if a less attentive general electorate holds contrary views. With the GMS, there appear to be "identity publics" worldwide, groups of people who identify fiercely with one identity that is often ignored by the majority of others in their society. This helps to explain some of the more counterintuitive findings on identity strength and the most important identities to global citizens. In most of the countries we surveyed, respondents rate themselves on average as being just as closely identified with their racial and ethnic identities as they are with their gender- and class-based identities. On this metric, one might

36 CITIZENS OF THE WORLD

conclude that racial identity is just as important globally as gender and class identities. Yet when we look instead at the identities that are *most important*, we find that a sizable minority in the United Kingdom, Australia, New Zealand, and Chile feel a strong sense of kinship with those of the same gender, far above what we find for race or ethnicity. Similarly, in South Korea class is one of the more important societal divisions, especially among older citizens. While these "identity publics" may constitute only 10% to 15% of the overall population, the strength with which they identify with their gender or class may play a pivotal role in which issues receive the greatest legislative attention.

Discussion

In this book, we examine eight countries across six continents, each of which has unique characteristics that drive political and social behavior among citizens. The salient identities vary across these contexts, and identities such as race, ethnicity, and nationalism may not have the same meaning in each country or exert the same influence on political behavior. Yet despite the diversity of the population we examine, there are critical similarities in the way Millennials view themselves that differ from older generations. This indicates that both global and domestic politics are likely to evolve in predictable ways as Millennials and post-Millennials grow in political power and influence. While there is suggestive evidence in the GMS that identities such as race and gender have grown in importance for younger generations, the key finding is that Millennials have thrown off the shackles of restrictive labels that differentiate in-group members from out-group members. Millennials are less likely to say they feel a subjective sense of attachment with almost any label as strongly as older generations do, with the notable exception of "citizen of the world." Nationalism, although it remains the single most salient identity, is not nearly as important for Millennials as it is for non-Millennials.

In place of nationalism, we find a greater sense of cosmopolitan identity. The tension between cosmopolitanism and patriotism is well-documented by theorists concerned with the policy implications of excessive patriotism and nationalism. Nussbaum (1996) suggests that individuals who feel stronger connections to those belonging only to the same family, community, race, religion, or nationality may be more motivated to prefer policies that favor those groups over others. This discriminatory behavior can have negative consequences for the welfare of minority groups. The literature on social identity provides further evidence that individual citizens react in this way, showing greater in-group preference and out-group antipathy when they view politics through their racial or partisan identities (e.g., Huddy 2001; Jardina 2019; Mason 2018). Nussbaum (1996) herself proposes a cosmopolitan identity as a normatively desirable alternative to patriotism, though she has since revised her position as favoring a "globally sensitive patriotism" (Nussbaum 2008). Both philosophies urge citizens to think beyond sectarian lines and avoid falling into traps in which patriots define themselves as substantially different from outsiders. While this line of thinking is not without critics (see, e.g., Papastephanou 2013), the normative implications of nationalism versus universalism are clear. A universalist can be characterized as idealistic, yet the Millennial generation appears far more likely than their predecessors to embrace that governing philosophy. And although the findings here do not suggest that a sense of patriotism or nationalism will be completely displaced by a cosmopolitan sense of identity, we do find evidence that suggests Millennials view policy through a more universalist lens, which we discuss in greater detail in the next chapter.

Despite these findings, we recognize that this shift toward cosmopolitanism and a rejection of more exclusive labels among Millennials may be an age effect rather than a cohort effect; that is,

Millennials' attitudes toward a cosmopolitan identity may change as they grow older. We are unable to definitively answer this question without data that track this generation across their lifespan. The idealism we have uncovered early in life among Millennials may eventually erode as future events and life experiences influence political attitudes and Millennials' self-conception. Despite this, Millennials are unique in that they came of age during a period of globalization on both economic and technological fronts, which should have lasting effects on the way they view themselves and their governing philosophies for a global society. Only time will tell whether Millennial citizens will use their cosmopolitan sense of identity to shape world politics.

3

Millennials as Digital Natives

News Consumption and Political Preferences

The internet and the social media revolution have fundamentally changed the way news is transmitted to the masses. This change in the news industry has disproportionately affected Millennials. The Millennial generation is the first to be considered digital natives, meaning most of this cohort grew up only knowing what it is like to have instant communication or immediate information at their fingertips (Rouse and Ross 2018). As a result, Millennials have enjoyed access to and greater familiarity with the internet and social media (what we refer to here as "new media") and have relied more heavily on these sources for social and political news than older generations. For example, Millennials were the first generation to have access to Facebook and were the earliest adopters of Twitter and Instagram and other social media platforms.

Not only were Millennials the quickest to adopt these platforms as a source of news, but surveys consistently show that they and the younger Generation Z are the most likely to rely on these sources to inform their political opinions (Pew Research Center 2019). The internet revolution strongly influences the way journalists now approach their jobs. Scholars show that journalism has shifted in recent decades toward more subjective, opinion-based reporting. Even those individuals relying on more conventional forms of print journalism and television for political news encounter journalistic styles that have shifted from straight reporting on facts and events to subjective and argumentative styles of reporting (Kavanagh et al. 2019).

Citizens of the World. Stella M. Rouse, Jared McDonald, Richard N. Engstrom, Michael J. Hanmer, Roberto González, Siugmin Lay, and Daniel Miranda, Oxford University Press. © Oxford University Press 2023. DOI: 10.1093/oso/9780197599372.003.0003

40   CITIZENS OF THE WORLD

As we discuss in this chapter, the shift from print and television journalism to internet and social media is not restricted to any one country or region but is a global occurrence with potential implications for political engagement and policy attitudes. To understand the impact of this shift, we need to first briefly discuss whether and how we distinguish between the internet and social media. Often, the internet is treated as a "black box" that encompasses various forms of communication, such as online news, email, messaging applications, and social media (Zhuravskaya, Petrova, and Enikolopov 2020). Social media as a source of political news represents an important shift from offline media due to lower barriers to entry and greater reliance on user-generated content (Zhuravskaya, Petrova, and Enikolopov 2020). These low barriers to entry make it more difficult to control the spread of (political) information, and therefore allow many newcomers that were previously blocked by the political establishment to challenge traditional interests and forms of communication (Loader and Mercea 2011). In this chapter, we outline recent changes in media consumption and discuss how these changes disproportionately affect members of the Millennial generation. We then discuss the threat misinformation poses in the modern decentralized media landscape.

In outlining the results of the Global Millennial Survey (GMS), we show that Millennials are more likely to report using the internet or social media as their top source of political information and that Millennials' preferences for new media are relatively consistent across countries compared to older generations, who are more likely to have distinct preferences based on their country context. Interestingly, we do not find evidence that younger individuals or those relying on new media believe they struggle to separate fact from fiction when consuming political news. Instead, we find large percentages of *all* respondents across all countries expressing concern about their ability to find accurate political information. These findings suggest that citizens may not be concerned specifically about misinformation on social media or the internet but may worry more generally about the reliability of any news source.

Turning to political interest, we find that non-Millennials are moderately more interested in politics than Millennials, though overall interest remains high. Those in this cohort who have the greatest political interest disproportionately rely on the internet as a source for news. We conclude the chapter by investigating the ways policy preferences are related to an emerging Millennial identity informed by news consumption. Although some analyses are constrained by sample size considerations, they serve as a starting point for future research into the relationship between generational cohorts, media consumption, and policy preferences from a comparative perspective.

Millennials as the New Media Generation

In the context of American politics, research shows that younger citizens are especially likely to shirk print and television journalism, instead opting for online news where incidental exposure to certain types of news stories is less likely (Zerba 2011). For example, someone who normally lacks interest in foreign policy, but who regularly watches a general news program on a media outlet such as CNN or the BBC, may be unable to avoid becoming at least somewhat informed about the state of foreign affairs. On the other hand, someone who goes to CNN.com or BBC.com is presented with options to skip stories related to foreign affairs, leaving them underinformed on that topic. Lower levels of incidental exposure linked to the increased use of online news sources may partly explain why younger cohorts overall consume less news than older cohorts (Kohut 2013).

Alternately, the proliferation of (mostly free) news sources on the internet and social media means there are many sources of nonpolitical news, allowing individuals who prefer not to follow politics to opt out of political news entirely. Research shows that, with the growth of social media, interest in political news has declined, while interest in other types of news has remained steady or increased (Ha et al. 2018). The availability of political news, it seems, is a necessary but not sufficient condition for ensuring a well-informed and engaged society. Information overload and information choice in the internet age can lead some citizens to avoid political news entirely.

The proliferation of online news also raises questions about the potential for bias in the types of news citizens consume. Unlike the traditional nationally broadcast television and radio news programs along with local newspapers that dominated the media landscape throughout the twentieth century, new media sources allow consumers to cultivate an information environment suitable to their preferences. A growing body of research finds that online news consumption and political discussion are polarized and segregated based on individuals' predispositions, creating echo chambers rather than a diverse array of news sources one can use to become better informed (Flaxman, Goel, and Rao 2016; Jacobson, Myung, and Johnson 2016; Kuklinski et al. 2000, 2001; Mutz 2006; Pariser 2011; Shirk 2010). Yet other studies note that, although social media sites may expose a small minority of internet users to politically extreme and biased websites, the most popular websites are mainstream. Those who use the internet for political news tend to consume a wide variety of media sources, making them especially likely to come into contact with perspectives with which they disagree (Dubois and Blank 2018; Nelson and Webster 2017). Antunovic, Parsons, and Cooke (2018) find that young citizens frequently engage in "routine surveillance" of the news, receiving regular news updates via mobile apps or email from trusted sources, but that they also receive news incidentally through social media sites like Twitter or Facebook—sites they normally rely on for information outside of political news but which still contain large amounts of political content.

That younger people rely on multiple sources and platforms for political news is, on the one hand, encouraging as it suggests they are less likely to take any individual piece of information at face value. Yet the finding that social media may direct individuals to news sites even when the individual is not specifically looking for political news raises questions about the veracity of such sites and the potential for misinformation. Incidental exposure of political news from reputable news sites should not be worrisome, but this research shows that the incidental exposure among younger citizens tends to occur on social media. Social media networks are found to be ideologically homogeneous (Lönnqvist and Itkonen 2016), so any misinformation shared online is likely coming from a source who shares similar values with the consumer.

Disinformation and Misinformation

The growing reliance of many on the internet and social media for news has important implications not only for the types of stories people see but also the veracity of those stories. Despite a high reliance on the internet for sources of news, a 2019 Reuters Institute and University of Oxford report found that only 11% of individuals across nine countries had paid subscriptions to any online news content (Newman et al. 2019). Filling the void are free news sites that rely on high internet traffic, creating an incentive for news stories and headlines that generate "clicks" (i.e., "clickbait," or entertaining news that does not have the same journalistic rigor of a mainstream news source). While disinformation (information that is false) is problematic, scholars also point to the rise in political misinformation (information that is known to be false but is disseminated to achieve a political goal), which has grown in recent years online and threatens the healthy functioning of democracies (Lazer et al. 2018; Lewandowsky, Ecker, and Cook 2017; van der Linden et al. 2017; van der Linden, Panagopoulos, and Roozenbeek 2020).

44 CITIZENS OF THE WORLD

There are a number of characteristics of average citizens that are relevant to a discussion of misinformation. Citizens are not often deeply interested in all facets of political life, leaving them uninformed about many areas of politics and policy (Delli Carpini and Keeter 1996). They may not only avoid information that runs counter to their predispositions and attitudes (Kuklinski et al. 2000, 2001), but they may even reject information that runs counter to their views, justifying this by categorizing those news stories as bad or unreliable (Hopkins, Sides, and Citrin 2019; Swire et al. 2017). These features are not specific to Millennials, but they may be especially problematic among any group that is exposed to a wide variety of news sources and stories, as they may be incentivized to look for information that confirms the opinions they hold are "correct."

Scholarly research to date is mixed on whether misinformation can be corrected (see, e.g., Berinsky 2017; Gerber and Green 1999; Nyhan et al. 2019; Nyhan and Reifler 2010; Nyhan, Reifler, and Ubel 2013; Porter and Wood 2018; Prior, Sood, and Khanna 2015), though there is no doubt that greater exposure to the falsehoods that proliferate online presents a challenge for democratic governance. Therefore, it is worth systematically exploring where Millennials around the world obtain their news. If Millennials are getting their news online and, most especially, from social media sites that only recently began policing the veracity of their stories, it follows that Millennials may have greater difficulty locating accurate information or distinguishing real news from false stories.

Global Millennial Survey: Where Do People Get Their News?

Turning to the results of the GMS, we first present our findings on the sources of political news Millennials and older cohorts turn to. For this analysis, we asked respondents in all eight countries to rank their top five sources of political information: the internet, social media, television, newspapers, and radio. We focus here on which source was listed first, as it can be expected to be the primary source of political information, though we do not preclude the possibility that important political information could come from a second or third choice.

We find that, in large part, both Millennials and non-Millennials across the globe list the internet as their top source of political information (Figure 3.1). As discussed previously, the literature on political information finds that internet sources tend overwhelmingly to be legitimate journalistic sources of news, but they provide customers greater flexibility to cultivate their own news feeds, such that they can read only particular types of stories or stories focused on certain topics. In all eight countries surveyed, Millennials were more likely than non-Millennials to choose the internet as their top choice, though the differences were negligible in South Africa and South Korea. In six of the countries surveyed, the differences were greater than 10 percentage points, including the United States, where more than 50% of Millennials named the internet as their top choice for political information, but less than 34% of older respondents did the same.

A similar dynamic is found for reliance on social media. In seven of the eight countries, Millennials were more likely to name social media as their primary source of political information. Only Chile bucks this trend, though here the differences are small, and Chileans overall show a low preference for social media as their primary source of political news. Roughly a quarter of Millennials in the United States, the United Kingdom, and Australia say social media is their primary source of news. Differences in Australia between Millennials and non-Millennials were especially drastic, as 24% of Millennial Australians listed social media as their top source of news, but only 5% of older Australians relied primarily on social media.

Outside of new media, television was far and away the most popular source of political news, with non-Millennials especially

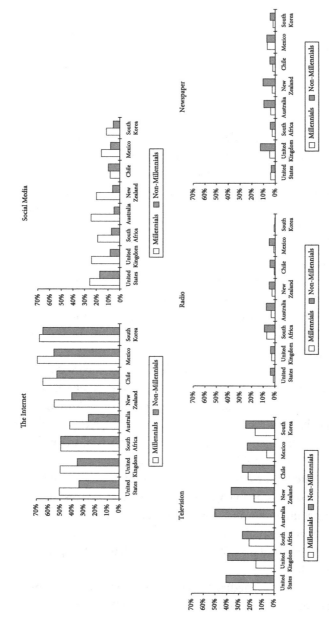

Figure 3.1 Top Source for Political Information, by Age Group

preferring television news over other sources. In the United States, the United Kingdom, and Australia, majorities or near-majorities of respondents over age thirty-five said that television was their top source. On average, non-Millennials were 16 percentage points more likely to rely most heavily on television for political news.

Across both Millennials and non-Millennials, usage of both newspapers and radio as primary sources for news was exceedingly low. Although non-Millennials said they rely on radio for political news more than Millennials did, no group in any country included in the GMS had more than 10% point to radio as their primary source of information. Print media was slightly more popular, especially among non-Millennials in the United Kingdom and New Zealand, though these percentages indicate that only a small proportion of the population looks to print media primarily for political information.

The evidence here is consistent with research finding that younger people are disproportionately reliant on new forms of media for political news. Reliance on the internet and social media reinforces the global identity that defines Millennials, described in the previous chapter. Figure 3.2 shows a breakdown of reliance on new media (internet and social media) separated by Millennials and non-Millennials. These results highlight two important findings. First, strong majorities of Millennials in all eight countries rely on some form of new media for political news, while older cohorts are far less reliant on these new technologies. Television remains the dominant source of political information for a large proportion of non-Millennials but is losing its influence among the younger portions of the public. Second, Figure 3.2 highlights that Millennials not only have higher average scores of new media usage than the older cohort (75.78% select the internet or social media as their primary source of news, compared to 53.64% among non-Millennials), but also varies within a much narrower range (a 17-point range, from 68% to 85%, compared to the older group's 40-point range, from 31% to 71%). The fact that Millennials not only

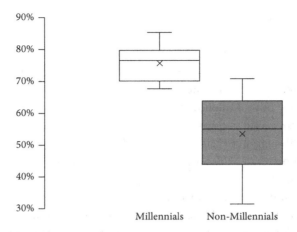

Figure 3.2 Variation in Generational Use of New Media as the Primary News Source

use new media more frequently than older cohorts but also cluster together in terms of their preference for news sources provides evidence consistent with the notion of the "global Millennial citizen"; older cohorts are defined more by country differences, while Millennials have preferences that are more like one another across national boundaries. When it comes to media consumption Millennials are indeed displaying preferences that suggest a global identity with behaviors and attitudes that are better understood as generational rather than preferences structured by their home countries.

Assessing the Difficulty of Separating Fact from Fiction in News

Given the Millennial generation's proclivity for and reliance on new media for political news, we seek to determine the degree to which misinformation threatens their ability to understand the news accurately and come to informed political opinions. This is important because Millennials will soon be the largest worldwide generation and will control many political, social, and economic institutions across the globe. Understanding the difficulty of discerning truth from nontruth is particularly important for the future of democratic governance. However, assessing belief in falsehoods is a fraught exercise in any academic study due to the challenge of determining what constitutes a falsehood—a problem that is made even more difficult in a comparative setting where the quantity and context of disinformation can vary. In an effort to avoid making subjective judgments about what is true or false, or whether examples of misinformation are comparable across countries, we opt for a more straightforward survey tool: asking respondents whether they find it difficult to separate fact from fiction when reading political news.

Based on the findings of the GMS, Millennials do not find obtaining accurate information more difficult, though important caveats exist (Figure 3.3a). Despite the large gaps in how people obtain their news, the gaps in the difficulty of finding accurate information are smaller and less predictable. On average, the gap between Millennials and non-Millennials on the difficulty of finding accurate information is less than 2 percentage points. Yet in places like the United States and South Korea, large gaps exist. In the United States, non-Millennials are more than 13 percentage points more likely to say that finding accurate political information is difficult. In South Korea (and to a lesser extent, the United Kingdom), the pattern is reversed, with Millennials expressing frustration at separating fact from fiction. Liberals in the South Korean government have, in recent years, sought to combat "fake news," which may imbue a concern about misinformation with an ideological valence (*New York Times* 2018), so we are cautious not to overinterpret these differences as stemming from sources of political information. What is consistent, however, is that concern about news accuracy is high regardless of country or age group. Majorities in all

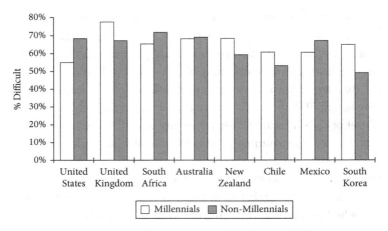

Figure 3.3a Percentage of Respondents Who Report Difficulty Getting Accurate Political Information, by Age Group

Note: Percentages represent "somewhat difficult" and "very difficult" combined.

eight countries said that finding accurate information was either "somewhat" or "very" difficult, with majorities much higher in a number of the countries.

This finding, however, does not appear to be related strongly to the source of information on which people rely (Figure 3.3b). If anything, individuals who rely on new media report finding it slightly less difficult to locate accurate information. In five of the eight countries surveyed, new media users reported lower levels of difficulty in getting accurate information than those using more traditional forms of media, like television, newspapers, or radio. Yet on average these differences were modest (less than 4 percentage points), suggesting few important differences between news source and perceived difficulty in acquiring accurate information. Taken together, these results suggest that, although Millennials rely heavily on new media sources where misinformation is a threat, this young cohort generally believes it is capable of discerning the accuracy of the information.

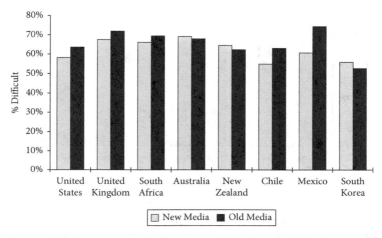

Figure 3.3b Percentage of Respondents Who Report Difficulty in Obtaining Accurate Political Information, by Top News Source

Note: Percentages represent "somewhat difficult" and "very difficult" combined.

In addition to asking respondents how difficult it was to find accurate political information, we asked specifically whether they found it difficult to find political information online. These findings provide further support to the hypothesis that both Millennials and non-Millennials self-select into the sources of news they trust are accurate. Differences in most countries are relatively modest (Figure 3.4a). When we examine the difficulty of getting political news based on the respondents' preferred news source (Figure 3.4b), we find that new media users report locating accurate news online to be much easier. Consistently, we find little evidence of a link between the preference of Millennials for the internet and social media and perceptions that it is harder to separate fact from fiction. Those who rely primarily on television, newspapers, or radio for news may express difficulty finding accurate information online, but this itself may explain why they avoid getting their political news online. Unfortunately, testing whether Millennials are actually better than non-Millennials at discerning fact from fiction

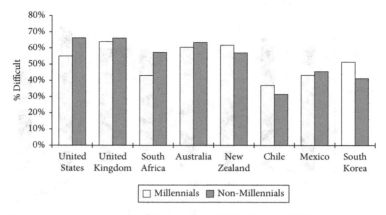

Figure 3.4a Percentage of Respondents Who Report Difficulty in Obtaining Accurate Political Information from the Internet or Social Media, by Age Group

Note: Percentages represent "somewhat difficult" and "very difficult" combined.

in their political news consumption is beyond the scope of this project. Therefore, we are careful to draw conclusions about the ability of respondents to differentiate between accurate information and misinformation. It may be that self-selection or preference for certain online news sources makes it more difficult for individuals to cast a critical eye on the information they are consuming. Future research should examine if there is a generational and/or country-specific component to how new media is acquired, how it is interpreted, and the way it is further disseminated.

How Do Media Preferences Relate to Political Interest?

Thus far, we have shown that younger citizens consistently prefer new forms of media such as online sources and social media to keep up with political news, and that these sources may contribute to a

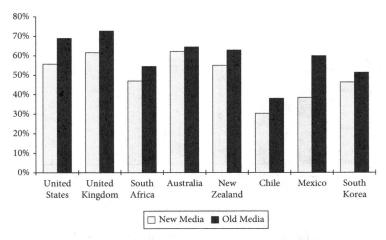

Figure 3.4b Percentage of Respondents Who Report Difficulty in Obtaining Accurate Political Information from the Internet or Social Media, by Top News Source
Note: Percentages represent "somewhat difficult" and "very difficult" combined.

global Millennial worldview. These preferences, however, do not have a consistent relationship with the degree to which Millennials or older cohorts perceive difficulty finding accurate political information. We now turn to the question of political interest. As we noted previously, many studies find that the proliferation of news online and via social media is not itself problematic among highly engaged individuals, who tend to read a variety of sources and stick primarily to mainstream journalism. First looking at levels of political interest, we note the troubling global trend that Millennials are generally less interested in the political world than older generations (Figure 3.5a). The data show that Millennials in seven of eight countries are less likely to say they are following politics somewhat or very closely.

Is political interest related to the types of news sources individuals seek? In Figure 3.5b, we show the preferred source of political news among Millennials and non-Millennials, separating

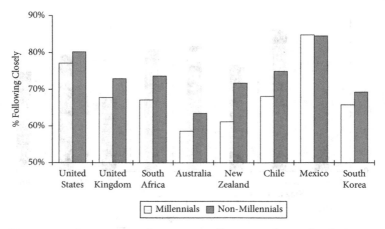

Figure 3.5a Percentage Who Report Following Politics Closely, by Age Group
Note: Percentages represent "somewhat closely" and "very closely" combined.

those who are the most politically engaged from those who are less engaged. For purposes of statistical precision, we combine all respondents regardless of their country. The results show that the internet is overwhelmingly the preferred source for political news among all respondents, but especially for those who are most engaged with the political world.

Social media is the second most popular source among Millennials, but the difference between highly engaged respondents and those less engaged is relatively small. With the proliferation of news sources on social media, people have greater ability to opt into sources that provide them with the content they want, which often means finding news that reinforces their previously held opinions. We find that the most politically engaged Millennials are not necessarily gravitating toward social media. Based on the existing research on media preferences and political knowledge (e.g., Ha et al. 2018), it seems that a significant portion of relatively unengaged Millennials are opting to use social media but are likely

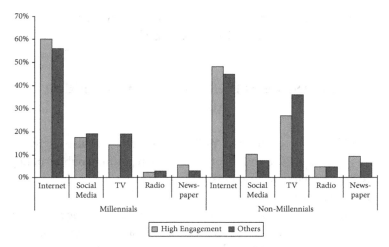

Figure 3.5b Preferred News Source of Those Following Politics Who Are Highly Engaged Compared to Those Less Engaged

not seeking out political information. This finding points to a potential danger because low-interest Millennials may be susceptible to misinformation campaigns due to untrustworthy news stories being shared by people within their own social network. Despite this, we cannot say with any certainty that Millennials actually buy into the falsehoods they may be exposed to on social media, and the results from the previous section do not suggest that these respondents find it especially difficult to separate fact from fiction online. Among non-Millennials, this trend is reversed, with the more highly attentive individuals choosing social media for political news slightly more often.

The only other popular source of political information was television, which was disproportionately preferred by lesser-engaged individuals regardless of age. These results seem to fit the picture of a global citizenry where highly engaged individuals gravitate toward online sources that provide them with a high volume of political news and the ability to customize the content they see, while

56   CITIZENS OF THE WORLD

lesser-engaged individuals rely on the news they happen to come across while surfing the web or watching television.

How Do Media Preferences Relate to Political Attitudes?

In addition to examining political interest, we also examine the answers to a number of questions regarding public policy preferences. Here we also look for evidence of a global identity that drives greater homogeneity in policy attitudes among Millennials than among older respondents. The items we rely on gauge attitudes on topics that were sufficiently common in all eight countries and for which we could accurately measure the opinions of respondents. We focus on three questions in particular: we asked everyone to rate (on a 1–5 scale) (1) if they were on the side of more or less government spending, (2) if they preferred government-provided healthcare or no government intervention on healthcare, and (3) if they generally thought diplomacy or armed action was the best tool in foreign policy (i.e., a hawk vs. dove measure). We then classified individuals as being on one end of the scale or the other, and those who selected the middle of the scale were classified as neutral. The results in Figures 3.6–3.9 represent the percentage of respondents who supported more government spending, greater government involvement in healthcare, and diplomacy, respectively.

The data show that Millennials overall tend to be less supportive than non-Millennials of increased government spending, government-provided healthcare, and diplomacy-first foreign policies. Moreover, there is evidence of a global Millennial identity that shapes these views. In most countries, a plurality of respondents supported more government spending (Figure 3.6a). In five of eight countries, non-Millennials were more supportive of increased spending, with gaps especially noteworthy in Australia, New Zealand, Chile, and South Korea. The reverse is seen in South Africa,

MILLENNIALS AS DIGITAL NATIVES 57

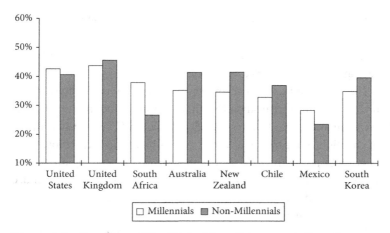

Figure 3.6a Percentage Who Prefer More Government Spending

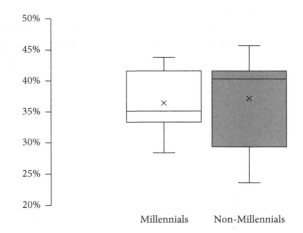

Figure 3.6b Variation in Generational Preference for Government Spending

where Millennials were 9 percentage points more likely to see government spending as the correct course of action. The results also indicate that Millennials across the globe tend to look more like each other than non-Millennials do (Figure 3.6b). Across all eight countries, support for greater government spending among Millennials stayed within a roughly 15-point range (28.36% to 43.73%), while the range among non-Millennials was 22 percentage points (23.60% to 45.61%).

Pluralities or majorities in most countries preferred government-provided health insurance to other options, though support was lower in the United States and South Korea (Figure 3.7a). In six of the eight countries surveyed, non-Millennials were more supportive of government-provided healthcare, though again the reverse was the case in South Africa, where Millennials were more supportive of government intervention. Once again, Millennials were more consistent in terms of their opinions across the globe (Figure 3.7b). Millennial approval for government-run healthcare stayed within a 16-point range, while non-Millennials varied by a 24-point margin.

Among respondents in our sample, diplomacy was the strongly preferred course of action (relative to the use of armed force), but Millennials showed a great deal more comfort with armed action

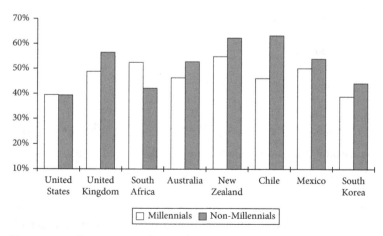

Figure 3.7a Percentage Who Prefer Government-Provided Healthcare

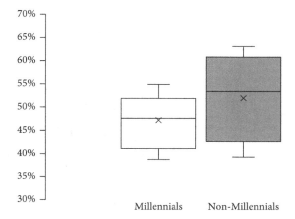

Figure 3.7b Variation in Generational Preference for Government-Provided Healthcare

than non-Millennials did, with the exception of the United States (Figure 3.8a). Here, the variation from country to country by age is more similar, though the overall range for Millennials (21 points) is substantially smaller than the range for non-Millennials (32 points).[1]

That policy attitudes vary a great deal based on Millennial/non-Millennial categorization is noteworthy, but we also examine whether these differences are conditioned by respondents' preferred sources of news (Figure 3.9). For this analysis, we again combined the samples across countries to increase statistical precision and focused on the top three sources of political news: the internet, social media, and television. We therefore consider this analysis speculative and urge future research to better assess the causal relationship between news sources and the policy views of younger and older generations in a comparative setting.

On the issue of government spending, we find that Millennials who rely on television for political news were most supportive of more government spending. Among non-Millennials, however,

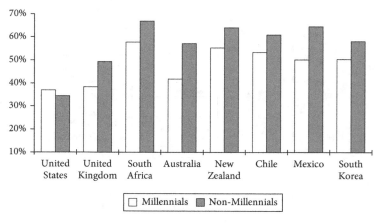

Figure 3.8a Percentage Who Favor a Diplomacy-First Approach to Foreign Policy

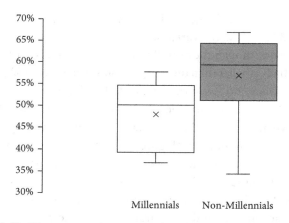

Figure 3.8b Variation in Generational Preference for Diplomacy

it was those respondents who used social media who expressed greater support for more government intervention.

On government-provided healthcare, differences across news sources were modest. Millennials who relied on social media and

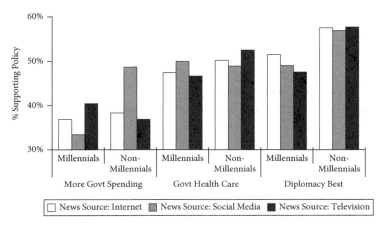

Figure 3.9 Policy Attitudes by Main Source of News, by Age Group

non-Millennials who relied on television were the most supportive of government-provided healthcare, but the differences are relatively small, suggesting that news source is not particularly influential on preferences regarding healthcare.

On the question of preferred approach to foreign policy, Millennials were differentiated by who uses new media. Those relying on the internet and social media were more likely to adopt a diplomacy-first approach (i.e., dove stance) than those relying on television. This finding speaks to the global identity of Millennials and the important role of new media (and new technology) in the understanding of that identity. It seems that Millennials' preference for new media, which provides an easier connection to those outside one's country, may lead to greater preference for discussing and working out disagreements with other countries rather than engaging in military action. For non-Millennials, however, the source of news mattered far less for preferences in their approach to foreign policy.

Diverging policy preferences based on age may stem from a multitude of factors, so we are hesitant to make causal claims. Yet the results displayed in Figures 3.6–3.9 let us explore the contours

62   CITIZENS OF THE WORLD

of political ideology and an emerging global Millennial identity. It is noteworthy that, outside of the United States and South Africa, Millennials exhibited a preference for a more constrained form of government. Work in the U.S. context finds Millennials to be significantly more liberal than older cohorts (Rouse and Ross 2018), a finding that the GMS shows does not fully extend to other countries. Moreover, the finding that Millennials are less likely to endorse the dove perspective on foreign policy presents some worrying implications about the prospects for peace in the future. In most of the countries surveyed, Millennial preference for a diplomacy-first approach hovered only around 50%. And across all three policy attitudes, the range of preferences for Millennials was narrower than the range among older groups. Millennials from different parts of the world appear to share far more in common with each other than non-Millennials do. This is likely shaped by the common sources of political news on which they rely. While this potentially opens the door for more effective global cooperation in the decades to come, the responses to our question on foreign policy suggests the need for more research.

Discussion

In this chapter, we have presented evidence consistent with previous research on news consumption of differing age cohorts. Millennials are more reliant on the internet and social media for their political information—sources that suffer from relatively higher levels of misinformation. In half of the countries surveyed, more than three-quarters of Millennials said they relied on the internet or social media as their top source of political information, and in no country was reliance among Millennials on new media less than two-thirds.

However, Millennials do not appear to find it more difficult to separate factual information from disinformation. In fact, new media users report less difficulty on average finding accurate political information. Although we cannot say for sure that new media users are actually receiving accurate information, the evidence here is consistent with a citizenry that picks the sources of political news they believe offer the most accurate information.

In terms of political interest and policy attitudes, important variation exists between Millennials and non-Millennials. Millennials are less interested in politics and less in favor of government intervention in the economy and healthcare. Across several policy attitudes, Millennials not only differ from non-Millennials, but they also appear to hold similar views across the different countries. These trends suggest that Millennials have cultivated a global identity, often sharing more in common with each other than they do with older compatriots.

This chapter's finding that Millennials express less interest in politics is a concerning one with potentially severe implications for democratic governance moving forward. In the next chapter, we more fully explore the question of political engagement among Millennials and non-Millennials across the globe. Consistent with the notion that Millennials are somewhat disinterested in politics, we find that Millennials are less likely to engage in common political activities such as voting. Yet this does not mean they are disaffected from public life entirely. As the findings in this chapter show, substantial majorities of Millennials say they follow politics and have preferences about the way government should operate, but they choose different methods for becoming informed. Similarly, we show that Millennials choose to engage in the political system in less traditional but equally important ways.

4

How (Politically) Conventional Are Millennials?

Exploring Preferences for Varying Forms of Political Participation

Political participation is a cornerstone of the modern democratic system. From liberal conceptions, which put voting as the center of political involvement, to republican cosmopolitan and/or critical notions, which consider broader ways of involvement, all types of democracies recognize the relevance of citizens' political participation (Della Porta 2013). In that sense, political participation and democracy are inseparable (Van Deth 2014).

However, currently there are two main forms of political participation around the world that have been particularly prominent during recent decades. One is conventional political participation, or "duty-based citizenship" (Dalton 2015), such as voting in national and local elections and involvement in political parties, which has been declining. In fact, from 1945 to 2015 voting has decreased by more than 10% in the world (IDEA 2016), even though the number of eligible voters has increased significantly during the same period. The other is "engaged citizenship" (Dalton 2015), the involvement of citizens in mass mobilizations and collective action (i.e., events with more than 100,000 people) aimed at promoting social change around the globe (Castells 2015; Nwanevu 2020). This less conventional form of political participation has been increasing. Indeed, between 2009 and 2019 there was an average yearly increase in mass mobilization of 11.5% (23.8% in sub-Saharan Africa, 18.9%

Citizens of the World. Stella M. Rouse, Jared McDonald, Richard N. Engstrom, Michael J. Hanmer, Roberto González, Siugmin Lay, and Daniel Miranda, Oxford University Press. © Oxford University Press 2023. DOI: 10.1093/oso/9780197599372.003.0004

in South America, 17% in North America, 16.5% in the Middle East and North Africa, 12.2% in Europe, 9.9% in Asia, and 4.9% in Oceania; Brannen et al. 2020).

Low participation in political parties and in democratic elections deteriorates the relationship between citizens and the state (Whiteley 2011). Low participation of this kind also erodes the role that political parties play in articulating the preferences of civil society to the state. Likewise, the election of representatives with low citizen participation weakens representatives' legitimacy. In addition, low levels of citizen participation violate the ideal principles of democracy (e.g., one person, one vote), since those who participate may have different interests than those who do not (Gilens 2012; Verba et al. 1995).

Throughout the field of democratic political thought, researchers have defined and redefined what qualifies as political participation. Before the 1940s, the focus was on voting as the main form of political activity. In the 1950s, there was an expansion toward understanding other conventional activities such as participation in political campaigns or contacting representatives. By the 1970s, there was a shift toward understanding social mobilizations and protests as other forms of political activism. In the 1990s, social activities and civic participation were integrated into the conception of political participation. Since the expansion of the internet, activities carried out on social networks have been considered forms of political activities (Chayinska et al. 2021, Theocharis 2015; Theocharis and Van Deth 2016; Van Deth 2014). This reveals the rapid expansion and permanent challenge of defining citizens' repertoire of political actions that allows them to get involved in public life.

There are several ways to conceptualize political participation, from narrow to broader conceptions. On the one hand, Verba, Nie, and Kim (1978, 2) define it as "those activities by private citizens that are more or less directly aimed at influencing the selection of government personnel and/or the actions they take." On the other

66 CITIZENS OF THE WORLD

hand, Van Deth (2014, 351) considers it an "activity, that is done by people in their role as citizens, that it should be voluntary, and that it deals with government, politics, or the state in the broad sense of these words." Despite multiple definitions, all efforts to capture political participation recognize at least two core aspects: (1) an institutional, formal, or conventional form of participation and (2) an activist, nonconventional form of participation (Albacete 2014; Ekman and Amnå 2012; González et al. 2021; Miranda et al. 2020; Zukin et al. 2006). Formal participation refers to those activities carried out by citizens within formal institutions, such as voting or formally enrolling in political parties. Activist participation, on the other hand, refers to a set of civic behaviors conducted outside of the institutions, aimed at influencing the political system (pressure to change the development of a particular law, to influence public opinion or a parliamentary voting, etc.; Van Deth 2014; Miranda et al. 2020).

Considering that there are at least two forms of political participation—duty-based citizenship and engaged citizenship—it is feasible that different people do not participate in the same way. Indeed, there are clear generational differences in political participation. Typically, younger people tend to abstain from participating in more conventional forms of political actions such as voting (Smets and van Ham 2013; Dalton 2015) but tend to engage more in nonconventional forms of participation than older people, such as activism (González et al. 2021; Norris 2011; Rouse and Ross 2018). These generation-based differences have led to the questioning of how citizens of different cohorts perceive, evaluate, and act in the political arena (Neundorf and Smets 2017), highlighting the importance of understanding the intergenerational differences.

The Millennial Generation has attracted particular attention in recent decades. This generation, born between the early 1980s and late 1990s (see Chapter 1), is skeptical about the functioning of several democratic institutions but shows a greater orientation toward nonconventional forms of political actions and more openness to embracing global goals. Given these marked characteristics, the transformative potential that this particular generation has in various nations of the world has been pointed out as an important topic to address (Zachara 2020). In this chapter, we first describe conventional (voting) and nonconventional (activism) forms of political participation of Millennial (age thirty-four or less) and non-Millennial (thirty-five or older) participants from the eight countries where the GMS was conducted (United States, United Kingdom, South Africa, Australia, New Zealand, Chile, Mexico, and South Korea). Then we compare Millennials and non-Millennials on several factors that have been considered in the literature to be predictive of these forms of political participation, such as citizens' interest in politics, political efficacy, and the importance citizens attribute to several forms of political behaviors. Finally, we discuss the important role these factors play in voting and activism participation, considering the implications for global society moving forward.

Conventional and Nonconventional Political Participation of Millennials and Non-Millennials

Millennial and non-Millennial participants in the GMS were asked to report their level of involvement in voting (conventional) and in nonconventional political actions such as signing a petition, taking part in a demonstration, attending a political meeting or rally, contacting politicians or public officials to express their views, donating money or raising funds for a political activity, and participating in internet forums or discussion groups to address political issues.

As previously discussed, involvement in formal or "duty-based" activities such as voting is one of the main political behaviors where differences between Millennials and non-Millennials have emerged. Research shows that younger people tend to participate less in conventional political activities than do older people (Smets and Van Ham 2013; Neundorf and Smets 2017; Rouse and Ross 2020; Zachara 2020), likely due to their disaffection from and critical views toward traditional forms of political participation.

As portrayed in Figure 4.1 and inconsistent with previous research, we first note that participants from all countries report high levels of voting in previous elections. However, it is noteworthy that this indicator captures self-reported voting turnout, which may exaggerate measures of turnout (e.g., Silver et al. 1986). In line with prior work, Millennials show lower rates of turnout compared

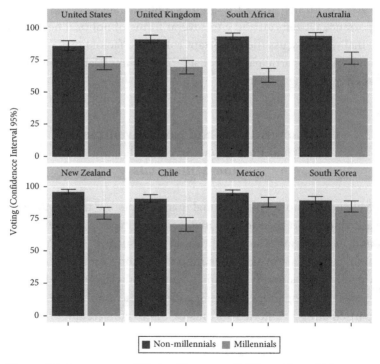

Figure 4.1 Percentage of Voting Turnout of Millennials and Non-Millennials, by Country

HOW (POLITICALLY) CONVENTIONAL ARE MILLENNIALS? 69

to non-Millennials in all countries except South Korea, where differences were modest. This difference was particularly strong in the United Kingdom, South Africa, Australia, New Zealand, and Chile, where variation in voting turnout between Millennials and non-Millennials ranged from 15% to 20%.

The other six measures are related to nonconventional or "engaged citizenship" forms of political participation. All of them, at different levels, aim to promote social change by influencing political processes in different ways. Based on previous theorizing and evidence (e.g., Smets and Van Ham 2013), we expect to find Millennials to be more willing to engage in these kinds of activities than their non-Millennial counterparts.

Signing a petition is the first nonconventional behavior we report. Although petitions are not always effective, they represent a low-cost activity. Signing a petition can take many forms, from support for a public statement or massive requests to change a current law. Examples are the multiple public declarations signed by citizens after the outbreak of Chilean social unrest that started in October 2019 and the written request of more than 6 million people to revoke the decision of the United Kingdom to depart the European Union, which was received by the U.K. Parliament after the 2016 referendum.

Figure 4.2a depicts the petition-signing rates reported by Millennials and non-Millennials. In most countries, more than 50% of respondents reported engaging in this behavior, except in Chile and South Korea, where the rate was below 50%. In addition, the results revealed significantly lower rates of petition-signing by Millennials than non-Millennials in three of the eight countries (South Africa, Australia, and New Zealand). In the remaining countries, no differences emerged.

The literature considers protests or demonstrations to be a form of collective action aimed at expressing discontent with the status quo and promoting social change (Somma et al. 2021; Van Zomeren et al. 2018). While young people are more likely to engage in this

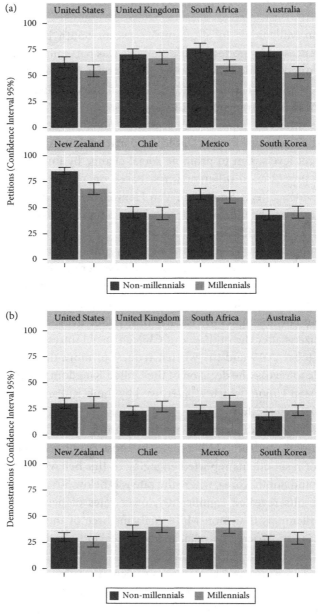

Figure 4.2 Percentage of Participation of Millennials and Non-Millennials in Signing Petitions (a) and in Demonstrations (b), by Country

HOW (POLITICALLY) CONVENTIONAL ARE MILLENNIALS? 71

form of participation, overall the participation of both younger and older adults is relatively low. Figure 4.2b displays reported rates of participation in demonstrations. About 30% of respondents reported engaging in this form of activity—at lower rates than voting and signing petitions (Figure 4.1 and Figure 4.2a, respectively). Although Millennials reported higher levels of involvement in demonstrations in seven of the eight countries surveyed, the differences between Millennials and non-Millennials tended to be small.

The reported rates for attending political meetings or rallies are presented in Figure 4.3a. Participation in this form of activity was rather low; only 25% of participants in most countries reported having attended political meetings or rallies, except in the United States, South Africa, and Mexico, where participation was relatively higher. Furthermore, differences between Millennial and non-Millennial participants in all countries were modest except in Mexico, where Millennials reported higher participation than their non-Millennial counterparts.

Figure 4.3b reveals the percentage of people who declared having contacted politicians or public officials to express their views. Again, Millennials reported significantly lower levels of this behavior than non-Millennials, this time in the United States, Australia, and New Zealand. Differences between the two groups in the remaining countries were smaller.

Donating money is another form of political participation. Figure 4.4a displays citizens' participation with regard to financial donations. Participants across all countries exhibited low levels of donating or fundraising. In three countries, South Africa, Australia, and Mexico, Millennial participants reported significantly higher levels of this form of participation than non-Millennial respondents. In the other countries, differences between the two groups were more modest.

The activity in which young people are especially more likely to be involved is the use of social media networks for political purposes.

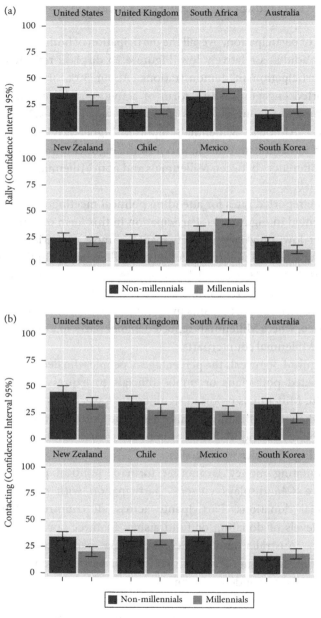

Figure 4.3 Percentage of Participation of Millennials and Non-Millennials in Attending Political Meetings or Rallies (a) and Contacting a Politician or Public Official (b), by Country

HOW (POLITICALLY) CONVENTIONAL ARE MILLENNIALS? 73

The internet has been widely used to spread messages and opinions, to foster social interactions, and to participate in social protest and social movements (Gainous et al. 2013). Given its proliferation and the multiple options it offers to engage with the political system, there is currently an important discussion about the role that on-line actions play in fostering the development of democratic systems across the globe (Chayinska et al. 2021). We observed that in South Africa, New Zealand, Chile, and Mexico, participation rates in internet forums or group discussions to address political issues were significantly higher among Millennial than non-Millennial participants (Figure 4.4b). In the remaining countries, Millennials still engaged at higher rates, but the differences were smaller.

Building an Index of Activist Participation

To create a single index of activism and to distinguish formal and informal forms of participation, we estimated a set of tetrachoric correlations.[1] First, voting—our formal behavioral measure—showed the lowest association with the other forms of participation (ranging between $r = 0.14$ and $r = 0.36$). In addition, the less formal indicators—the activist behavioral measures—were associated among themselves (ranging between $r = 0.50$ and $r = 0.60$), except the "signing a petition" measure, which was less associated with them (ranging from $r = 0.32$ to $r = 0.44$). This pattern reveals that voting indeed operates as a different form of political participation, compared to the other measures. Thus, the indicator of activist political participation, ranging from 0 to 6, considers the activist political actions that respondents carried out without considering voting since the latter reflects formal political participation.

Figure 4.5 depicts the indicator of activist political participation by country. Contrary to expectations, we observe no major differences between Millennial and non-Millennial respondents except in Mexico, where Millennials reported a higher level of

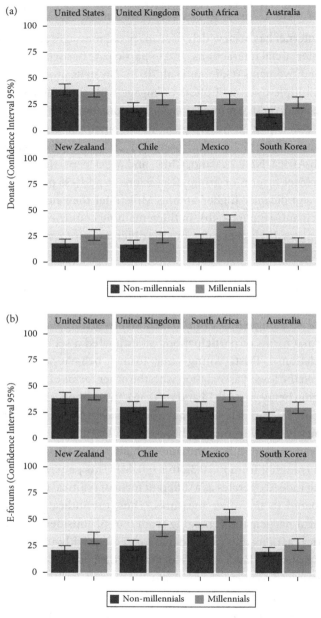

Figure 4.4 Percentage of Participation of Millennials and Non-Millennials in Raising Funds or Donating for Political Activities (a) and in Internet Forums (b), by Country

HOW (POLITICALLY) CONVENTIONAL ARE MILLENNIALS? 75

activist participation than their older counterparts. Importantly, voting was weakly but positively associated with the activist indicator in almost all countries but Mexico and South Korea.

Predictors of Voting and Activist Political Participation

Having described how Millennials and non-Millennials differ in terms of both their voting behavior and activist political participation, we now turn our attention to some critical factors that are often related to these political outcomes.

Based on previous research, we focus attention on three main concepts: (1) citizens' interest in politics (how closely they follow politics), (2) political efficacy (the extent to which people feel they could do as good a job in public office as others, and have a good understanding of the important political issues facing their country), and (3) the importance people attribute to different political behaviors such as voting, activist participation, and participation in political organizations. These concepts are relevant since they are shown to predict both formal and informal types of participation.

Political Interest and Political Participation

A key point of discussion about Millennials relative to non-Millennials is whether they are interested in and care about politics at all. Political interest is usually defined as the desire of people to pay attention to politics (Almond and Verba 1963; Lupia and Philpot 2005). Most conceive of political interest as an individual and quite stable attribute (Van Deth and Elff 2004) that might depend on the specific skills or resources of individuals. Moreover, young people generally have fewer skills and resources than older adults (Holbein and Hillygus 2020). However, recent theorizing

76 CITIZENS OF THE WORLD

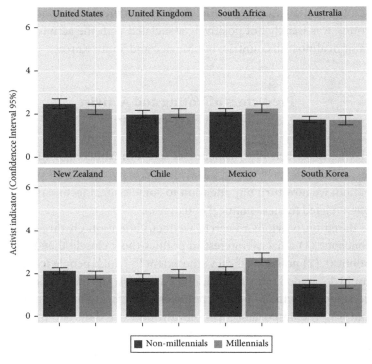

Figure 4.5 Overall Activity in Nontraditional Forms of Political Activity, by Country

(Silvia 2006) based on the appraisal theories of emotions (Lazarus 1991; Roseman and Smith 2001) has expanded that view and proposed that interest could be conceived on the same level with emotions such as fear and sadness. Emotions stem from the cognitive evaluations of events individuals experience; in the same fashion, interest in political issues could emerge as a consequence of the appraisal individuals make of the political system. Silvia integrates these two theoretical traditions by suggesting that political interest can be understood not only as an individual's subjective experience but also as a stable individual characteristic (Weinmann

HOW (POLITICALLY) CONVENTIONAL ARE MILLENNIALS? 77

2017). Consistent with this view, interest in political issues has been defined as the degree to which politics arouses citizens' curiosity (Van Deth 1990 or as an affective behavioral motive (Koestner and Losier 2002).

People interested in politics know more about the political system and are more likely to vote and participate in politics (Delli Carpini and Keeter 1996; Masullo Chen et al. 2020; Richey and Taylor 2012; Smets and Van Ham 2013; Verba et al. 1995). As Russo and Stattin (2017) point out, citizens who are politically interested have the motivation and skills to learn about political issues, making them more likely to search for political information (Silvia 2008; Strömbäck and Shehata 2010). Thus, they can be regarded as more politically knowledgeable and sophisticated (Eveland and Scheufele 2000). Moreover, individuals who are politically interested are also more likely to be mobilized and influenced by those who want them to engage in political actions (Brady et al. 1995; Finkel 1985). Thus, they are active and motivated to start political discussions and feel efficacious about changing their society (Bennett et al. 2000; Craig et al. 1990). They also frequently engage in different forms of both offline and online political actions (Best and Krueger 2005; Verba et al. 1995). Being interested in politics, therefore, reveals the psychological engagement that individuals have with politics and their concern with public issues (Brady et al. 1995). Because of the strong link that exists between political interest and citizen engagement, one might assume that the democratic system could gain significantly by having citizens interested in politics.

According to Russo and Stattin (2017), contemporary democracies face two main challenges. First, not all people think that politics is interesting. For instance, the European Social Survey (ESS Round 6 2012) found that only 44.6% of respondents are interested in politics; a similar picture emerges in the United States, where 40.7% of the population is interested in politics (ANES 2014). Second, as Prior (2010) showed, interest in politics is stable, so it is

78   CITIZENS OF THE WORLD

unlikely that those who currently lack interest in politics will develop an interest in the future. This is one reason individual levels of political participation are so stable. People either vote often or abstain regularly, depending on their interest in politics (Gerber et al. 2003; Plutzer 2002). Shani (2009) studied the stability of political interest using panel data from the Youth-Parent Socialization Study (Jennings and Niemi 1974, 1981). Results showed high stability of political interest over time among participants when assessed at eighteen, twenty-six, thirty-five, and fifty years old, a finding that is consistent with Prior's (2010) results.

Do Millennials and non-Millennials exhibit similar levels of political interest, and to what extent do patterns emerge across the world? Previous work suggests that age is an important factor predicting levels of political interest and a wide variety of political activities (Glenn and Grimes 1968; Highton and Wolfinger 2001; Rosenstone and Hansen 1993). While interest tends to be stable for individuals, the extent to which it varies across generations is important to understand, especially as Millennials become a larger part of the electorate.

As depicted in Figure 4.6a, the results reveal that participants from all countries exhibited significant levels of political interest (measured by how closely they follow politics, that is, attention): above the midpoint (2.5) of the 1–4 scale, where higher values indicate more political attention. Respondents from the United States and Mexico exhibited the highest levels of political interest, and participants from the remaining countries showed levels surrounding the midpoint of the political attention measure. Few major differences emerged between Millennials and non-Millennials across all countries in terms of their political attention. Broadly speaking, participants from all the countries considered in this study were genuinely interested in politics, a finding that does not fit the perception of those who think that Millennials are far less interested in politics than people who belong to older generations.

Political Efficacy and Political Participation

Efficacy beliefs are central in human functioning and are critical for changing social reality (Bandura 1977; Van Zomeren et al. 2013. Political efficacy corresponds to the sense of competence in the political sphere, the feeling that one is capable of understanding how the political system works and influencing relevant political decisions, and the extent to which individuals believe that their actions can influence states' decisions (Almond and Verba 1963; Beaumont 2010; Campbell et al. 1954; Reef and Knoke 1993).

Individuals are more likely to participate in politics if they believe their political actions can be effective and spur social change. That is, when they see themselves as competent(the internal efficacy dimension) or when they are confident that the system will be responsive to them (the external efficacy dimension) they will be more likely to participate (Easton and Dennis 1967; Iyengar 1980). In this chapter, we focus on internal efficacy of Millennials and non-Millennials.

Political efficacy has been acknowledged as a powerful predictor of political participation (Abramson and Aldrich 1982; Finkel 1985; Hadjar and Becker 2007; Reichert and Print 2017; Verba et al. 1995), and some scholars have conceived it as a stable psychological resource (Milbrath and Goel 1977; Verba and Nie 1987; Rosenstone and Hansen 1993). Others have noted the importance of understanding that political efficacy can change as a function of psychological processes and external structural or institutional factors. For instance, Valentino and colleagues (2009) argue that internal efficacy shapes the emotional reactions that individuals might experience when facing policy threats. Under threat, citizens who feel confident about their ability to participate are more likely to act based on the feelings of anger that emerge. Participation therefore reinforces internal efficacy, especially when participation is successful. Because it is positively related to political engagement, political efficacy is usually viewed as desirable for the stability of

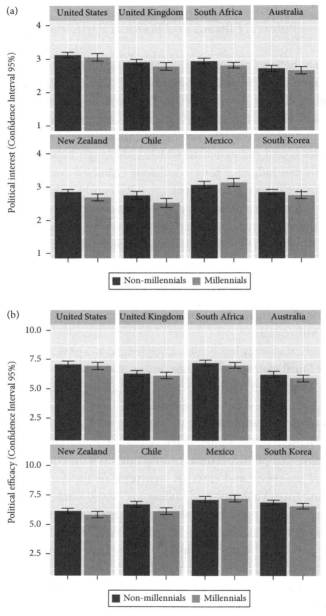

Figure 4.6 Political Interest (a) and efficacy (b) of Millennials and Non-Millennials, by Country

democracy. The more efficacious individuals feel, the more they might feel they have the power to influence decisions in the political arena (Wright 1981).

Reichert (2018) emphasizes the importance of political efficacy as an additional psychological factor when understanding political behavior (see also Levy and Akiva 2019). Using the German Longitudinal Election Study, he confirmed the central role political efficacy has when predicting intentions to participate in party politics—a political activity that requires a high degree of commitment (Ajzen 1991)—and nonconventional political behavior. Based on the dual pathway models (Strack and Deutsch 2004), Reichert (2018) argued that political efficacy should be associated with a rational political decision-making process (see also Reichert 2017), while political interest should be associated with motivated decision-making processes. Thus, political interest should be considered a more impulsive path for political decisions. It is therefore feasible that political interest is associated more with unconventional (e.g., participating in demonstrations, attending political meetings or rallies) than with conventional (voting) forms of participation.

Should we expect Millennials and non-Millennials to differ in their level of internal political efficacy? On the one hand, and based on the fact that political interest differs across age groups (Glenn and Grimes 1968; Highton and Wolfinger 2001; Rosenstone and Hansen 1993), we might expect to find variations in political efficacy between Millennials and non-Millennials. This expectation assumes that these two constructs can be associated and that the more people participate in politics, the more efficacious they feel in political terms (Valentino et al. 2009). Indeed, the association between age and political efficacy has been supported previously in research (Baker 1973; Hayes and Bean 1993; Marx and Nguyen 2016).

As portrayed in Figure 4.6b, in absolute terms participants from all countries exhibited intermediate levels of internal political

82   CITIZENS OF THE WORLD

efficacy, surrounding the midpoint (5) of the 1–10 scale, except for participants from the United States, Mexico, and South Africa, who in general showed higher levels of political efficacy, above the midpoint of the scale. Similar to the results for political interest, no difference emerged between Millennials and non-Millennials across all countries in terms of their political efficacy, except in the case of Chile, where Millennials exhibited significantly lower levels of political efficacy compared to non-Millennials. Broadly speaking, participants from all countries reported feeling somewhat efficacious in terms of their ability to influence the political system and promote change.

Perceived Importance of Different Forms of Political Participation

Last, but not least, we discuss the importance that Millennials and non-Millennials attribute to several forms of political participation. The importance that respondents attribute to these behaviors could reflect the extent to which they value democracy as a fundamental political system. Specifically, we investigate how important it is for Millennials and non-Millennials to vote in local and national elections, to engage in political activities aimed at changing local and national conditions, and to join local and national political organizations.

We reason that the perceived importance of these political behaviors is linked to the notion of good citizenship, which considers political participation a norm that shapes attitudes and behavior (Bolzendahl and Coffé 2009; Coffé and van der Lippe 2010; Jennings 2015). As previously noted, Dalton (2015) delineates two types of norms—duty-based citizenship and engaged citizenship—to explain differences in political participation among younger and older generations. Duty-based norms correspond to traditional forms of participation in politics, such as voting, paying taxes, and respecting the law—in other words, activities aimed at reinforcing existing political authority and order (Dalton 2015). If people are more likely to support duty-based norms, they will be much more willing to engage in the act of voting (Van Deth 2007) and be less likely to participate in nonconventional forms of political activity (Bolzendahl and Coffé 2013; Dalton 2015). These duty-based norms generally tend to be more common in older adults. Engaged citizenship corresponds to norms that are aimed at promoting social change and reducing inequalities. Those who embrace engagement-based norms participate more often in volunteerism, boycotts, demonstrations, and other forms of contentious actions—activities that emphasize more direct participation of government and policy (Rouse and Ross 2018). Young people hold stronger engagement-based norms than duty-based norms when compared to older groups (Dalton 2015; Rouse and Ross 2018).

We examine Millennials' and non-Millennials' preferences for forms of political participation. The findings described earlier in this chapter suggest that Millennials may be less likely to attribute importance to voting, since they reported lower levels of voting behavior. However, the opposite may emerge regarding the importance they attribute to being engaged citizens. As portrayed in Figure 4.7a and consistent with earlier results, participants from all countries attributed much importance to voting, expressing values above the midpoint (5.5) of the 1–10 scale.

These results reveal a consensus about the value of engaging in this conventional form of political participation. Furthermore, important differences emerge when comparing Millennials and non-Millennials. Specifically, Millennials attributed less importance to voting compared to non-Millennial respondents in almost all countries. This difference is in line with the systematic and significantly lower levels of voting reported by Millennials in comparison to non-Millennials in the current study (see Figure 4.1). A different picture emerges when we examine the importance

84 CITIZENS OF THE WORLD

respondents place on participating in activities attributed to engaged citizenship (Figure 4.7b). First, respondents in the United States, followed by Mexico, South Africa, and to a lesser extent South Korea, expressed higher levels of importance to political activism (above the midpoint of the scale). Respondents in the remaining countries—the United Kingdom, Australia, New Zealand, and Chile—expressed medium levels of perceived importance of political activism in absolute terms (around the midpoint of the scale). Moreover, Millennials attributed greater importance to engaging in political activism compared to non-Millennials, with differences especially pronounced in the United Kingdom, Australia, and New Zealand.

Examining the importance participants place on joining local and national political organizations, we see differences in priorities compared to voting and engaging in political activism. Figure 4.7c shows that participants from Chile, New Zealand, and Australia attributed rather low levels of importance to joining political organizations. In contrast, citizens of the United States, followed by citizens of South Korea, South Africa, Mexico, and the United Kingdom, showed, in relative terms, higher levels on this dimension. Moreover, and mirroring the differences observed in the importance Millennials and non-Millennials attributed to engaging in political actions aimed at changing the local and national conditions, we also observed significant differences in the importance they attributed to joining political organizations. Specifically, Millennials expressed greater importance in joining local and national political organizations compared to non-Millennials in the United Kingdom, Australia, and New Zealand; differences were smaller in the rest of the participant countries. These are the same countries that showed disparities in the perceived importance of engaging in activist political participation.

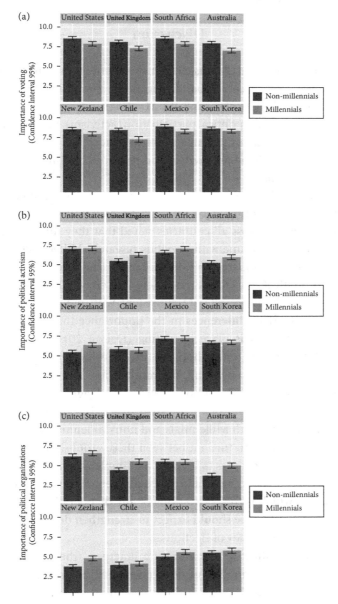

Figure 4.7 Importance of Voting (a), Engaging in Political Activism (b), and Joining Political Organizations (c) of Millennials and Non-Millennials, by Country

Discussion

The findings reported in this chapter shed light on the current theoretical and empirical discussion regarding conventional or duty-based forms of political participation (voting) and nonconventional or engaged forms of political participation (activism). Furthermore, we are able to examine related political concepts that allow us to compare the political preferences and priorities of Millennials and non-Millennials.

First, we demonstrate that participants from all countries exhibited high voting rates in previous elections (around 75% of participants across all countries stated that they turned out to vote). However, in line with previous research, Millennials voted at lower rates compared to non-Millennials in all countries, except in South Korea, where no differences emerged between the two groups. These results are consistent with previous research that demonstrates differences in the importance that Millennials and non-Millennials place on voting (Dalton 2015; Rouse and Ross 2018). By examining both reported levels of voting and the importance placed on voting, the results show that there is congruence between expressed preference for engaging in the act of voting and in the value placed on such an act. This high consensus is at play among both Millennials and non-Millennials despite reported differences in turnout between these groups. These results call on modern societies to identify and implement measures that foster greater engagement among young generations in electoral processes, which is the cornerstone of any democratic system. By reducing this gap, we should expect to strengthen democracy and increase the legitimacy of elections.

Second, a rather different picture emerged when comparing these two groups on several nonconventional forms of political participation. The results reveal less consistent patterns with previous research. On most measures of less conventional or "engaged citizenship" forms of participation (activism), results revealed little

HOW (POLITICALLY) CONVENTIONAL ARE MILLENNIALS?   87

or no differences across these groups, with the important exception of Millennials being more likely to make political donations or raising funds and participating in online political forums. When comparing a robust single index of activism—by aggregating all indicators except voting behavior into a single measure—the results revealed no difference whatsoever between Millennials and non-Millennials in all countries but Mexico. These results illustrate that these two groups may not be as different in many of the behaviors related to political activism as we previously believed.

Turning to the predictors of voting and political activism, participants from all countries, broadly speaking, exhibited high levels of political interest and moderate levels of internal efficacy. Here, no differences are observed between Millennials and non-Millennials on these dimensions except in Chile, where participants exhibited low internal political efficacy. We suspect that, at the time of the data collection, Chilean Millennials were experiencing disaffection and higher levels of political cynicism regarding the current state of Chilean politics, which could potentially have a negative impact on their sense of political efficacy. Again, these findings do not fit the perception that Millennials are far less interested in politics and feel less efficacious than people who belong to older generations. In fact, this is in line with research on Millennial political engagement in the United States that finds this generation to be equally if not more engaged in politics when compared to older adults (Rouse and Ross 2018). Some differences emerged, however, regarding the importance Millennials and non-Millennials attributed to both engaging in political actions aimed at changing the local and national conditions and joining political organizations. Consistently, only Millennials in the United Kingdom, Australia, and New Zealand attributed significantly more importance to these political actions compared to non-Millennials. The fact that these differences emerged in only these three countries poses a challenge to democracy. As we pointed out, for democracy to function properly, it is important to have an engaged citizenry.

Those who show an appreciation for multiple forms of participation may have greater efficacy about the functioning of their democratic system.

The current evidence reveals that Millennials are not strongly disengaged from the political system. Above and beyond the differences we reported in comparison to non-Millennials, Millennials were interested in politics, they attributed value to voting, they voted, and they felt quite efficacious when acting to express their preferences within the political system. Moreover, Millennials in the United Kingdom, Australia, and New Zealand attributed higher importance to engaging in political activism at the local and national level and to joining political organizations compared to non-Millennials. In other countries the differences were modest, though absolute levels of participation were still high.

Remarkably, our results also show that voting and activism are associated. That is, the more people vote, the more they get involved in political activism, although they capture two different types of political participation (conventional and nonconventional, respectively). Thus, both forms of political participation can reinforce each other and strengthen our democratic systems, particularly when those actions are oriented to promote social change.

5

Duty-Based Citizenship, Engaged Citizenship, or Somewhere in the Middle?

Millennials' Interest in Serving the Public

In the previous chapter, we discussed the importance of distinguishing between different forms of participation, particularly as they relate to the way Millennials engage with politics. However, engagement does not occur in a vacuum; other factors help determine whether and how it takes place. As we have argued throughout this book, it is important to understand how Millennials and older adults differ in terms of the way they obtain information and how they feel about their roles as democratic citizens. Democracy, after all, demands that ordinary citizens do the work of gathering information, forming policy preferences, connecting those preferences to the alternatives on the ballot, and holding elected officials accountable for their performance in office. We have shown that while modes of behavior might differ between Millennials and non-Millennials to some extent, the new wave of Millennial citizens are, in fact, not disengaged from the political system and are generally interested in being part of the democratic process.

The fact that Millennials around the world are markedly less interested in voting is perhaps the most striking finding in the GMS. In the previous chapter, we noted that Millennials are less likely to vote in elections, compared to their older counterparts. This is true in all eight countries surveyed by the GMS. This is not to say that

Citizens of the World. Stella M. Rouse, Jared McDonald, Richard N. Engstrom, Michael J. Hanmer, Roberto González, Siugmin Lay, and Daniel Miranda, Oxford University Press. © Oxford University Press 2023. DOI: 10.1093/oso/9780197599372.003.0005

they are abandoning the ballot box completely (reported voting rates remain high regardless of country or age cohort), but the act of voting does not have as much appeal to this younger generation of democratic participants.

Perhaps more comforting is the finding that, while the "duty-based" form of participating by casting a ballot is less attractive to younger citizens, they are still interested in engaging with political issues through more "active" means. Participating in demonstrations, donating money, and taking part in discussions are well-established components of democracy, and these forms of participation have already seen a resurgence due to the political engagement preferences of Millennials.

In this chapter, we explore another level of civic obligation that goes beyond the voting and activism that democracy demands of citizens: volunteering, joining local political organizations, and serving in government. These activities are immensely costly to individuals but are important for maintaining the welfare of communities more directly than voting in a national election or participating in an online forum. Furthermore, these activities can lessen the divide between "duty-based" and "active" citizenship in ways that have a durable impact on democratic governance (Rouse and Ross 2018). Democracies rely on citizens stepping up to serve their communities in both conventional and less conventional ways in activist organizations, elected offices, and bureaucratic roles that deliver government services. We examine whether Millennial attitudes are conducive to different forms of public service and whether there is a pipeline of young leaders interested in this type of political engagement.

Research shows that engaging in one's community is a result of establishing roots and feeling a sense of belonging (e.g., Putnam 2000; Campbell 2006). There is some concern that Millennials' attitudes and behaviors may not be conducive to building the permanency needed for at least some forms of local participation. Just as Millennials are comfortable moving from job to job (Adkins n.d.), early evidence shows that they are also likely to move from community to community

(Benetsky, Burd, and Rapino 2015). Furthermore, they are likely to delay the purchase of a home in a community (though this may be changing; see Lerner 2019) and are more likely to put off parenting (Livingston 2018). These dynamics change the typical relationships people have with schools, welfare programs, and other local services that focus on the quality-of-life needs of families. Decisions to live a more transient lifestyle suggest that Millennials, likely due to the changing nature of the workforce, see localities as temporary and therefore lack the motivation and resources to engage with the leadership and governance systems in their communities.

These trends have occurred in parallel with rising concerns about Millennials in the workforce. As new technology sectors become more prominent in the economy and pressures increase for workforces to be more mobile and adaptable, the expectation that workers will spend an entire career in the same location, or with the same company, has decreased considerably. Without a commitment to a place or even a particular company, corporate executives are concerned that Millennials will fail to nurture the next generation of company leaders (Adkins 2016). Millennial attitudes, it seems, may run counter to how companies have identified and recruited leaders in the past. For example, according to Gallup's 2016 report "How Millennials Want to Work and Live," new systems may have to be developed to encourage Millennials to step into leadership roles. Similar concerns about workforce stability may also affect public service and more community-based engagement.

Variation in the desire to fulfill public service roles has been studied for many years. Results from this line of research indicate that some groups of people have a higher level of "public service motivation" than others. Identifying citizens or public-sector workers with high levels of public service motivation, and figuring out how to encourage them to consider and pursue public service careers, has been a research focus in the public administration literature. Perry and Wise (1990: 368) define this as "an individual's predisposition to respond to motives grounded primarily or uniquely in

92 CITIZENS OF THE WORLD

public institutions and organizations." Since their study, others have examined how public service motivation varies by job type (Kim 2016), nationality (Van der Wal 2015), and demographic characteristics (DeHart-Davis, Marlowe, and Pandey 2006), making this line of research especially relevant to comparative studies of political attitudes, such as the present investigation.

Despite considerable research efforts and interest in identifying those citizens who are best suited for careers in the public service sector, there has not been conclusive evidence regarding the relationship between generational change and public service motivation. Yet it makes sense that large attitudinal shifts regarding government and how it should work could threaten norms that encourage people to seek out public-sector employment and pursue public service careers. After all, if Millennials increasingly view government institutions as being ill-suited to solve the problems facing society, it follows that they may be less motivated to occupy positions of power within public service organizations. Is it the case that the Millennial Generation has developed attitudes that make them less interested in serving in government, particularly at the local level?

Drawing from the literature on Millennial attitudes, we examine whether Millennials are less connected to local issues and communities and the political tools that exist at that level. We find that, despite the relative apathy Millennials express toward voting and more conventional forms of participation, Millennial respondents to the GMS *do* report being interested in local issues and in roles that extend to direct engagement with local politics and government.

Voting in Local Elections

We begin by revisiting the importance individuals place on voting and other conventional forms of participation, but we shift our focus specifically to the value citizens place on engaging with local government. Respondents to the GMS were asked a series of questions about engaging in politics at the local level. Of course, one of the ways to participate in a democracy is to cast ballots in local elections. Figure 5.1 reports the results for the importance placed on voting in local elections among our respondents.

Results for the importance of voting in local elections mirror those of participating in national elections: Millennials are consistently less interested in this particular method of engaging in democratic governance. Whether it is due to apathy about local issues and institutions or the belief that voting is an ineffective form of participation, and regardless of the type of election, local governments do not make the idea of voting any more appealing to Millennials.

Volunteering in the Community

Respondents were also asked to rate the likelihood of volunteering in their community. Figure 5.2 shows that, while there is variation from country to country, there is no consistent universal pattern that differentiates Millennials and older adults.

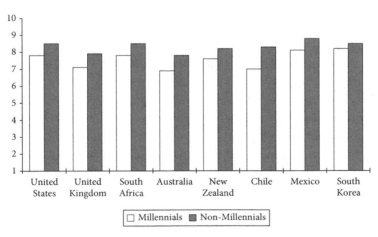

Figure 5.1 Importance of Voting in Local Elections (1–10 Scale)

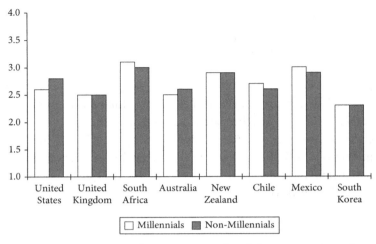

Figure 5.2 Volunteer in the Community (1 = "I have never done this, and would never do it"; 4 = "I have done this within the past year")

Millennials in three countries (South Africa, Chile, and Mexico) place more importance on local volunteerism, while non-Millennials in two countries (the United States and Australia) rank it as more important compared to the younger cohort. The three remaining countries report no difference between Millennials and older adults.

Although the differences on volunteerism are modest, it is important to note the way responses to volunteering in a community differ from the patterns related to voting in local elections. It would be inaccurate to describe Millennials as detached or disinterested in activities going on at the local level. Instead, Millennials are uniquely disinterested in the act of voting. These findings are therefore consistent with conclusions from the previous chapter. Engaging in activities that have a direct and local effect are relatively more attractive to Millennials than those activities, like voting, which may be perceived as more "duty-based" (even at the local level) and less directly connected to specific problems

Millennials want to address. Furthermore, the findings suggest that while Millennials may exhibit more transient tendencies than do older generations, they are still willing to engage in volunteerism. Is this also true for other types of local political activities?

Engaging in Local Political Activities

In addition to voting and volunteering, respondents were asked to rate how important it was to engage "in political activities aimed at changing local conditions." Asking respondents to think more generally about the local aspect of politics reveals an interesting pattern of responses across countries and cohorts. We report these findings in Figure 5.3.

In six of the eight countries, Millennials claim more interest in engaging in local political activities compared to non-Millennials. In several of these countries (namely the United Kingdom, Australia,

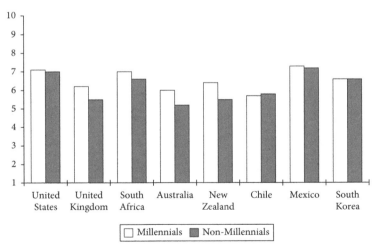

Figure 5.3 Importance of Engaging in Local Political Activities (1–10 Scale)

and New Zealand), Millennials are substantially more likely to view local political activities as especially important. This finding is in line with our conclusions from the previous chapter, where we showed that Millennials are more likely to participate in "engaged" rather than "duty-based" political activities such as voting. Only in Chile do non-Millennials have a (narrowly) higher level of interest in engaging in local political activities than Millennials, and South Korea reports no difference between the two groups.

Joining a Local Political Organization

Respondents were asked to rate how important it was to join a local political organization (Figure 5.4). This question captures a type of political activity that is more activist in nature but less individualistic than voting or volunteering, and one that is often narrowly focused on a particular issue or topic. When the object of the question

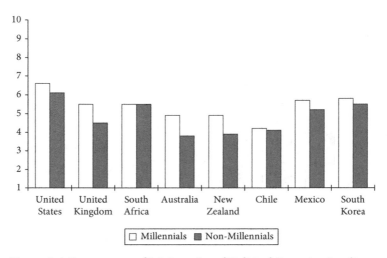

Figure 5.4 Importance of Joining a Local Political Organization (1–10 Scale)

shifts from voting or volunteering to engagement with a local political organization of the respondent's choosing, the results again show that Millennials are more interested in nonconventional forms of engagement with their local communities.

Figure 5.4 shows that in every country but one, Millennials place more importance on joining local political organizations. Again, Millennials in the United Kingdom, Australia, and New Zealand stand out. Non-Millennials in those countries exhibit some of the lowest overall levels of interest in joining local political organizations, but Millennials in those countries show significantly higher interest at levels similar to those seen in South Africa, Mexico, and South Korea.

The only country where Millennials do not rate joining a political organization as more important is South Africa, though even here there is no difference between Millennials and non-Millennials. This result, particularly when combined with the findings about engagement in local political activities, should ease concerns about Millennials being uninterested in local communities and not prioritizing the work that goes into local, democratic problem-solving.

Running for and Serving in Public Office

Figure 5.5 presents the results of the survey question that asked respondents how they felt about their ability to do a good job while in a public service role. This is perhaps the most direct question in the GMS regarding the extent to which we might have a leadership gap as older generations retire from elected and unelected public service roles. Simply put, if Millennials do not feel they can do the job of serving the public, there is little reason to suspect they will seek out those types of roles. Previous research has shown that Millennials in the United States are less likely to seek public office for a variety of reasons (Shames 2017). These include disillusionment

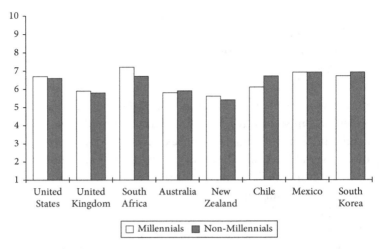

Figure 5.5 Agree with the Statement: "I feel that I could do as good a job in public office as most people" (1–10 Scale)

with the ability to enact change through government institutions, as well as a distaste for negative campaigns that expose personal information or simply spread lies about candidates. More recently, however, U.S. Millennials, especially women, have been more willing to enter the electoral arena. This is evidenced by the record number of women (225 as major party candidates) who ran for office in the 2018 midterm elections (Center for American Women and Politics 2019). How do Millennials around the world feel about their own ability to do the job of a public servant?

The results in Figure 5.5 do not show systematic evidence that Millennials feel any more or less qualified than others to serve in public service roles. In four countries (the United States, the United Kingdom, South Africa, and New Zealand) Millennials report feeling more qualified, while in three (Australia, Chile, and South Korea) they feel less qualified than do older citizens, and in one country (Mexico) there is no difference. Overall, then, there is little evidence to suggest that Millennials will shy away from public service jobs on account of their lacking the confidence necessary to do the job. Furthermore, when paired with the findings showing that Millennials are more engaged in local political activities, we find little evidence to substantiate the concern that Millennials will be disinterested in doing the work of local governance.

Discussion

Democracy requires that citizens not only cast a ballot or register a grievance with their governments but that they also fill information-gathering, problem-solving, and decision-making roles so that government is sufficiently staffed to perform its work effectively. The Millennial generation has garnered attention for this cohort's relatively unique workforce and lifestyle behaviors that tend to emphasize less commitment to long-term jobs and more transient residential patterns. These behaviors raise questions about their commitment to engaging in local governance. Initial results about Millennials' enthusiasm for voting, confirmed in this volume, reinforced some of these concerns. However, the uniqueness of the GMS allowed us to explore preferences beyond general voting attitudes. We asked respondents to consider their priorities related to engaging in the political problems that face local communities. Millennials expressed either as much or more commitment to participating in local political problem-solving activities and organizations compared to older citizens.

The results reported here examine the earliest phase of public service work: experience with and the perceived importance of volunteering and engaging at the local level. This examination is important because a vast majority of public servants begin their careers at the local level, where it is easier and less expensive to cut one's public service teeth. These initial results look promising for Millennials' engagement that may lie between pure "duty-based citizenship" and "active citizenship." However, it is still an open question as to whether or not Millennials will be sufficiently interested in solving local political problems to ascend to leadership positions within local organizations, local government, and eventually the national level. Future research will also have to determine the long-term effects of varying lifestyle patterns and career choices on political engagement. These behaviors are far from being mutually exclusive, and we have only begun to scratch the surface on how these choices, related more generally to the Millennial Generation identity, will influence this cohort's interest in both local and national politics.

6

Millennials

The Global Perspective and the Future of a Shared Generational Identity

The turn of the twenty-first century brought forth digital, technological, and communication advances that made human connections easy, instantaneous, and more direct around the globe. As "digital natives," Millennials are the first generation to grow up under this ubiquitous development. The exposure to these modern advances provided Millennials a different understanding of the world around them, one which allowed them to interact and feel a sense of greater belonging with all of humanity. It is no wonder, then, that Millennials, more than older generations, see themselves and are seen by others as global citizens. A generation whose members are citizens of the world should be examined through that lens.

The social sciences have long used generations as a way to categorize and understand cohorts. However, generations are most commonly examined within populations of a single country. This approach, while providing significant depth, comes at the expense of greater breadth and lacks a comparative perspective. For much of history it was perhaps less imperative that generational studies cross borders, as interactions around the world were much more difficult and infrequent. With this book, we hope to open avenues for future research using a more comparative approach, one that reflects the new realities of regular and easily accessible social interactions across borders.

Citizens of the World. Stella M. Rouse, Jared McDonald, Richard N. Engstrom, Michael J. Hanmer, Roberto González, Siugmin Lay, and Daniel Miranda, Oxford University Press. © Oxford University Press 2023. DOI: 10.1093/oso/9780197599372.003.0006

102 CITIZENS OF THE WORLD

Throughout this book, we have discussed a number of global circumstances and events that have disproportionately affected Millennials and united them (intentionally or unintentionally) on some level. These include formative events such as 9/11 and the war on terror, the Great Recession, and more recent crises like the COVID-19 pandemic and the protests for racial justice. The global protests for racial justice, in particular, are powerful demonstrations of the solidarity and interconnectedness exhibited by these global citizens. For example, in early June 2020, hundreds of mostly young South Korean activists gathered in Seoul to support the Black Lives Matter movement in the United States and to protest the killing of George Floyd. The protestors held signs and banners that read "Black Lives Matter" and chanted the slogan "No Justice, No Peace" (*Korean Times* 2020). Asked why the group felt compelled to hold the protest, the organizer of the event, Shim Ji-hoon (age thirty-four, a Millennial), said, "We want to show solidarity with the U.S. movement and remember Floyd who was sacrificed due to racism" (quoted in *Korean Times* 2020). Elsewhere he said, "Racism happens here in Korea. Whether they are from China, black or other immigrant workers, they are mocked and looked down on.... What happened to George Floyd can happen here too" (quoted in Strother 2020). Similar to the Arab Spring protests discussed in Chapter 1, the racial justice protests in South Korea and around the world demonstrate various elements of the Millennial persona— tolerance, justice, and a sense of cosmopolitanism—bolstered by the use of technology.

As we argue in this book, Millennials have a particular identity that characterizes their generation. This identity distinguishes them from older generations in two main ways. First, their identity is grounded in cultural norms and value shifts that are a product of experiences and events occurring at similar points in life (Rouse and Ross 2018). Second, their comfort with and use of technology is central to their persona and distinguishes them from older generations in terms of their global outlook. Therefore, it is imperative to meet Millennials where they are and explore their attitudes, beliefs, and political engagement from a universal perspective.

We have examined the Millennial Generation from this universal perspective for a number of reasons. First, this generation encompasses 1.8 billion people, a quarter of the world's population, and is the largest generation of adults around the world. In most countries, this cohort has already surpassed or will surpass Baby Boomers, previously the largest living generation and one whose members are "digital immigrants" (a generation that did not come of age with technological advances but acquired them later in life) rather than "digital natives" (Prensky 2001). Given their size and current age (the oldest Millennials are now in their late thirties to early forties), this generation will soon produce a majority of political, economic, and social leaders. These leaders are likely to chart the course for collective interests that will determine the stability of future institutions and the effectiveness of international cooperation. Second, given the implications of their influence, it is important to examine whether Millennial attitudes and beliefs are a product of country-specific factors or, as we expect, a more universal set of perspectives born out of core values, common experiences, and ability to communicate. For instance, as Rouse and Ross (2018) note, September 11, 2001, and the ensuing war on terror produced long-term consequences and helped frame for this generation how they think about the United States and the rest of the world. As we continue to study this, it is important to understand whether this global outlook is limited to Millennials in the United States or if it is more universal, determined by generational rather than country-specific factors. Finally, the ability to explore the current influence of Millennials and speak to their future power compels us to understand better what defines their persona, their various identities, their priority for change, and, if change is to take place, the tools they will utilize to make it happen.

Against the backdrop of global citizenship, we explored the political attitudes and behaviors of Millennials compared to older

104 CITIZENS OF THE WORLD

adults in eight countries: Australia, Chile, Mexico, New Zealand, South Africa, South Korea, the United Kingdom, and the United States. While we did not survey Millennials in every democratic country (a difficult feat), we are able to rely on a diversity of countries, across six continents, to identify with some confidence the extent to which this generation's attitudes and behaviors are similar to one another and distinct from older adults'. With this multicountry sample, we speak to a broad scope of issues that provides the first in-depth and empirical examination of how (global) generational identity can be distinguished and utilized to explain such factors as how news consumption shapes political attitudes, variations in levels and forms of civic engagement, and belief in one's ability to bring about political change.

Key Findings: Millennials as Global Citizens—Few Labels, Digital Ascendancy, and Nonconventional Engagement

Our initial task at the outset of this book (in Chapter 1) was to review what we know about Millennials to date, including previous work on the Millennial Generation identity, to convey the importance of examining Millennials on a global scale, and to establish the process by which we explore the attitudes and preferences of this generation. As mentioned above, in line with research that has focused on Millennials in the United States, we show that similar characteristics, circumstances, and experiences have affected this cohort around the world. In other words, there were no borders to the Great Recession, which disproportionately distressed the Millennial Generation in many ways and has shaped their outlook on politics and overall attitudes about democratic governance. This finding is perhaps even more important in light of the COVID-19 pandemic. Although our surveys were fielded prior to the onset of the pandemic, we believe the results should help inform future research into the consequences of the pandemic on the formation of political attitudes among younger generations of global citizens.

Millennials' characteristics, circumstances, and experiences raise two important questions: To what extent does this cohort in different parts of the world share values and policy preferences? What do these commonalities tell us about how they interact with the political world around them? To address these questions, we relied on public opinion surveys fielded in the eight countries included in our study. The survey questions tapped into issues about political and social divisions, political engagement, policy preferences, and approaches to solving problems. We gathered data from approximately six hundred respondents in each country, half of which were Millennials, and the other half older adults. This resulted in over three thousand responses across the eight countries, with variance on a number of important characteristics. These multicountry data allowed us to explore how disparate attitudes among Millennials and non-Millennials (older adults) about political, social, and economic norms influence issues of governance around the world.

In Chapter 2, we examined the core identities that characterize the Millennial Generation and how they are different from those that define older adults. One characteristic that we highlighted in this chapter was the increasing diversity of the population that is occurring not just in the United States but in many countries around the world. We argue that demographic change can affect citizens differently, depending on their generational cohort. These demographic shifts, along with other factors, help us better understand how Millennials and non-Millennials view themselves across the world and help shape these groups' policy attitudes and the ways they think about and engage with the world around them—both nationally and on the global scale.

The GMS allowed us to examine a number of salient identities. We asked respondents across the eight countries in our study to rate their level of attachment with eight different, potentially salient identities: national identity, cosmopolitan identity, racial identity,

106 CITIZENS OF THE WORLD

religious identity, ethnic identity, generational identity, gender identity, and class identity. We then asked respondents to select the identity that was most important to them.

In general, we found that Millennials, relative to non-Millennials, feel a subjectively weaker attachment to group-based identities. Millennials instead are more likely to identify with a cosmopolitan identity ("citizens of the world") compared to older adults. Overall, the strongest identity across all countries and age groups was nationalism—respondents identifying as citizens of their country. This identity was strongest for respondents in the United States and South Korea. Most compelling to our thesis of the importance of the Millennial Generation identity was the gap between this cohort and older adults. In almost every country, Millennials were less nationalistic than their elder co-citizens.

In this chapter we also explored which identities were most salient to both Millennials and non-Millennials. Although national identity is the strongest among both Millennials and non-Millennials, Millennials are much less likely to select nationalism as their most conspicuous identification. This is particularly true for Millennials in Australia, Chile, New Zealand, and the United States. We also noted the observed uniqueness of South Africa (among the countries in our study). South Africans have lower levels of nationalism, and it is the only country where Millennials display a relatively stronger sense of national identity. Overall, while a sense of cosmopolitan identity has not surpassed a nationalistic identity among Millennials, this cohort views itself much more as citizens of the world compared to non-Millennials. When respondents were asked to select which identity was most important to them, Millennials chose the cosmopolitan identity. This cohort was more likely to choose "citizen of the world" in seven out of the eight countries surveyed. This demonstrates a generational shift in terms of a sense of belonging—demonstrating that Millennials embrace a more culturally diverse and universal outlook.

We find mixed evidence for whether members of the Millennial Generation have a sense of group consciousness—an awareness demonstrated by individual group members about membership in the (generational) group. In all eight countries, Millennials express lower levels of generational identity compared to older cohorts. We argue that this may be because Millennials, in general, eschew group-specific labels. However, when forced to choose the single most important identity, in four of the eight countries— New Zealand, South Korea, the United Kingdom, and the United States—a greater percentage of Millennials chose their generational identity compared to older adults. We encourage future research to explore in greater depth and with expanded measures the strength of group consciousness among Millennials around the world.

Our results reveal inconsistent trends for both dispositional (e.g., race, ethnicity, gender) and situational (e.g., religion and class) identities. Respondents across the eight countries display a strong sense of race, ethnicity, and gender identities, but do not select any of them as most important. Similarly, religious identity is less important than national or cosmopolitan identities; however, in countries with a strong religious tradition, like South Africa and the United States, religion continues to play an important role, although older adults more so than Millennials motivate these findings. Class too tends to be a stronger identity for older adults, but it is not widely chosen as the single most important identity. Curiously, though, for a small number of respondents, all of these identities are shown to be particularly salient. We refer to these small portions of the citizenry as "identity publics"—a small group of society that is more likely to leverage a strong identity to engage in political activity. This is especially true for gender and class. While relatively few individuals prioritize these identities, those who do may be able to disproportionately influence both national and international policy decisions. It remains the case, though, that group-based identities are less import to Millennials than to older adults. Whether and how this continues to be a prominent feature as Millennials age will have important implications for global governance.

Chapter 3 fully engaged with the disparate Millennial/non-Millennial effects of the digital revolution and its effects on political interest and policy preferences. One of the most prominent themes throughout this book has been the digital and technological primacy of the Millennial Generation. In this chapter, we started with the premise that because of their early exposure (in their formative years), Millennials have relied more heavily on the internet and social media (i.e., "new media") as sources for social and political news. We argued that the tendency toward more subjective and argumentative journalism across these platforms has important implications for this generation. The shift from print and television journalism to the internet and social media was not limited to one country but rather was a global phenomenon, thereby raising important questions about how this evolution has influenced political attitudes and citizen engagement.

Once again utilizing the GMS, we were able to demonstrate that, not surprisingly, Millennials are more likely than non-Millennials to rely on the internet or social media as their top source of political information. Furthermore, we show that these preferences for news information among Millennials are relatively consistent across countries. In contrast, non-Millennials have more varying news source preferences, and these choices are more country-specific. The greater reliance on the internet and social media among Millennials and their consistent use that transcends country borders reinforce the global identity that defines the Millennial Generation. However, the inclination of Millennials to rely on new media does not come without drawbacks; primarily, this form of decentralized media landscape is ripe for the spread of misinformation.

Given Millennials' preference for the internet and social media, it was also important for us to explore whether misinformation creates an impediment to this cohort's ability to decipher the accuracy of news and reach informed political opinions. As the largest generation, and soon to be the most prevalent in positions of power, the ability to ascertain the accuracy of information has important implications for democratic governance. Our survey did not allow us to measure directly the accuracy of information consumed, but we were able to gauge whether Millennial respondents found it more difficult to find fact-based political news. We found that in all eight countries surveyed, there is great concern, regardless of cohort, for finding accurate news information. Only in the United States and South Korea did we find meaningful cohort gaps. In the United States, non-Millennials are more likely to say they have difficulty finding accurate political news, while in South Korea, Millennials find this task more challenging. Overall, although Millennials rely heavily on new media for political news, which is more susceptible to misinformation, this cohort believes it is mostly able to separate fact from fiction.

Despite their confidence in finding accurate news, Millennials around the world are generally less interested in politics than non-Millennials. While this trend is potentially troubling, it is not surprising; research has consistently shown that young cohorts tend to have less interest in the political world around them than do older adults (Rouse and Ross 2018). Is political interest linked to the type of news sources individuals seek out? We find that the internet is overwhelmingly the preferred source for news among all respondents, but it is especially preferred among those who are most politically engaged. The most politically engaged Millennials are not necessarily seeking out social media for political news. Instead, less engaged Millennials use social media, but not necessarily to find political information. The reverse is true for older adults: non-Millennials who are more politically engaged slightly prefer social media for their political news.

After we established that highly engaged individuals are more likely to seek out information online, we looked at the type of policy

110 CITIZENS OF THE WORLD

preferences that may result from a more globally connected citizenry. We asked survey respondents three policy questions that were common across all eight countries: preference for more/less government spending, preference for (or against) government-provided healthcare, and preference for diplomacy or armed action as a tool for foreign policy. Our findings revealed that Millennials overall are *less* likely than non-Millennials to support increased government spending, government-provided healthcare, and a diplomacy-first foreign policy. While some cross-country variation is observed, Millennials tend to have policy preferences that are more similar to one another than they are to their non-Millennial country counterparts. This is further evidence that Millennials' preferences are informed by a universal rather than country-specific identity.

We examined whether policy preferences are conditioned by a respondent's preferred source for political news. On this front, Millennials who relied on television as their primary source for news supported increased government spending. Among non-Millennials it was those who used social media who preferred greater government spending. We found modest differences on the link between news sources and support for government-provided healthcare. Millennials who primarily relied on social media for news and non-Millennials who primarily relied on television were more supportive of this policy, but the small differences suggest that news source does not strongly influence attitudes about the role of government in healthcare. Most interesting were our findings regarding news source preferences and attitudes about foreign policy. Millennials who use the internet or social media were more likely to prefer a diplomatic approach to foreign policy than those who relied on television. Once again, we see the importance of the global identity for Millennials. New media has supplied a digital bridge across the world. As this generation has more say in global governance, there may be greater opportunities to work out disagreements among countries rather than resorting to military action. Non-Millennials' news source had little effect on attitudes about foreign policy.

It is important to note that outside of the United States and South Africa, Millennials seemed to prefer more constrained government activity. Furthermore, only in the United States did Millennials, regardless of media source, prefer a diplomatic rather than military approach to foreign policy. This is consistent with research on American Millennials that has found them to have generally more liberal preferences toward government action and a more "dovish" approach to foreign policy (Rouse and Ross 2018). It may be that Millennials in the United States stand out on preferring greater government action because the baseline for such intervention has been lower than in most other democracies around the world. On the other hand, the United States has been engaged in military action for all or most of American Millennials' lives, with little success to show for it—a distinct experience, compared to that of Millennials in the other democratic countries we examine. As a result, Millennials in the United States appear to prefer an alternative and more diplomatic approach to foreign policy. Overall, more in-depth research is needed to better understand the variation in foreign policy attitudes of this generation across the globe.

In Chapter 4, we continued our evaluation of Millennials as global citizens by analyzing their role in the most consequential activity for a democracy: political participation. We distinguished between two forms of political participation. The first, known as "duty-based citizenship," involves such conventional participatory activities as voting and volunteering for political parties. The other, known as "engaged citizenship," refers to the participation of citizens in mass mobilization and collective action, with the goal of bringing about social change around the world. A less conventional from of political participation, engaged citizenship has increased in use around the world over the past decade. The growing popularity of engaged models of citizenship coincides with technological advances that allow individuals to communicate and participate

112   CITIZENS OF THE WORLD

on a global scale. As such, there is a clear generational difference in forms of engagement. Young cohorts tend to forgo conventional activities in favor of more engaged forms of participation (Rouse and Ross 2018). However, to date, there has not been much exploration of generational differences in political participation around the world.

In this chapter, we leveraged the GMS to examine both conventional and nonconventional measures of political participation. Respondents were asked to report their level of involvement in voting, signing a petition, taking part in a demonstration, attending a political meeting or rally, contacting politicians, donating money to political activities, and participating in internet forums to address political issues. With respect to voting, the most conventional measure of political participation, we found that respondents in all countries reported high levels of engaging in this activity. However, in all countries except South Korea, Millennials reported lower rates of turnout compared to non-Millennials. This disparity is in line with other research that has found lower levels of voting among Millennials (Rouse and Ross 2018). On measures of "engaged citizenship," we found both cross-country and Millennial/non-Millennial variation on levels of participation. Millennials were less likely to engage in petition signing in three of eight countries; in the other countries, few cohort differences emerged. In terms of contacting politicians or attending a political meeting, Millennials overall were less likely than non-Millennials to say they engaged in these activities, with a few countries displaying some modest cohort differences.

We know from previous research that Millennials, and young people in general, are more likely to participate in protests and demonstrations as a way to express their discontent with the status quo (e.g., Occupy Wall Street in 2011, Women's March in 2017, Climate Strike in 2019, Black Lives Matter in 2021). In our survey, we found that while participation in protests and marches overall is low (around 30% of respondents reported such participation),

Millennials in most countries reported higher levels of involvement in this activity than did non-Millennials, although the differences across cohorts were small.

In the era of digital technology, the use of social media networks for political purposes can either be a means to other participatory ends (calls for many protests and marches are first made or spread online) or an end in itself. The GMS found that Millennials do indeed engage at higher rates with social media networks than do non-Millennials. The differences were particularly stark in South Africa, New Zealand, Chile, and Mexico.

After discussing differences between Millennials and non-Millennials in "duty-based" and "engaged" citizenship forms of participation, we turned our attention to considering factors that may help predict these participatory choices. Guided by previous work, we focused on three measures: how closely citizens follow politics, political efficacy (defined as the extent to which individuals feel they could do as good a job in public office as others, and have a good understanding of the important political issues facing their country), and the importance people attribute to certain political behaviors. These measures predict both conventional and nonconventional forms of participation. In terms of political interest, we found few differences between Millennials and non-Millennials. Generally, participants from all eight countries reported being genuinely interested in politics. These findings dispel some of the perception that Millennials are not interested in politics.

It is an accepted principle of democratic governance that individuals are more likely to participate in politics if they believe their actions have some effect on the process, and therefore can bring about change. Did we find differences in political efficacy between Millennials and non-Millennials? In short, we did not. Similar to our findings on political interest, few distinctions emerged between these cohorts and across the countries. One exception was Chile, where Millennials reported lower levels of political efficacy compared to non-Millennials. In general, though, most

114   CITIZENS OF THE WORLD

respondents in our survey, regardless of whether or not they were members of the Millennial Generation, reported feeling somewhat efficacious about their ability to influence the political process.

The final mediating factor on political participation that we considered was the importance that individuals place on certain types of political behavior. Specifically, we looked at the importance of voting in local and national elections, of engaging in political activities aimed at changing local and national conditions, and of joining national political organizations. We posited that the perceived importance of these behaviors speaks to the idea of good citizenship that deems political participation an important norm. Respondents in all countries attributed great importance to the act of voting, but the importance of this behavior to Millennials was substantially lower than for non-Millennials in almost all countries. This was not the case when we examined the importance placed on political activism. Respondents overall expressed high to medium levels of importance on activism, but Millennials more than non-Millennials placed greater value on this behavior. This was especially true for Millennials in the United Kingdom, Australia, and New Zealand. Respondents displayed much more variation on the value they placed in joining political organizations, with a number of countries viewing this behavior as low in importance. However, Millennials reported higher levels of importance in joining political organizations compared to non-Millennials, with a greater gap in importance between these two cohorts in the United Kingdom, Australia, and New Zealand.

The Millennial/non-Millennial differences in levels of importance placed on these varying political behaviors underscore the preferences in participation among these cohorts. Millennials prefer activities that focus on "engaged citizenship," a less conventional but more active form of participation that brings people together in efforts of mass mobilization to highlight the need for rapid social change. On the other hand, non-Millennials prefer activities that are more "duty-based" and conventional and which in many ways are designed to reinforce the status quo or bring about more incremental change. It is not the case, then, that Millennials abstain from voting due to a lack of efficacy; rather, they view less conventional forms of political activity as more worthwhile efforts.

In Chapter 5, we examined the Millennial Generation's willingness to assume public service roles, specifically those in local political organizations. This analysis extended the discussion about what forms of engagement Millennials prefer and are willing to undertake. As we noted, Millennials find more conventional, "duty-based" forms of political participation (e.g., voting) in general less appealing compared to nonconventional, more "active" forms of engagement (e.g., protests and marches). However, whether and how their predilection for public service fits into these two participatory categories had not been previously explored. Furthermore, if Millennials fully eschew engagement with government institutions, this has important implications for the norms that inspire public service.

We also prefaced the importance of examining public service by discussing the fact that a common theme in public discourse has been concern over the transience of Millennials, who on average do not hold the same job or live in the same locality for as long as members of older generations do. These dynamics have the potential to weaken social bonds in communities, making these "global citizens" less invested in the welfare of issues at the local level, and perhaps less willing to engage with lower-level governance. These civic activities are more costly than other activities but are vital to maintaining the well-being of communities and to the overall health of democracy.

Leveraging questions in the GMS that tap into the value citizens place on engaging at the local level, we found that Millennials remain less likely to vote in local elections compared to older adults. The results were relatively consistent across all eight countries and underscore that Millennials are less interested in this form of participation, regardless of the level of government. We

116 CITIZENS OF THE WORLD

did find cross-country variation, but not a general pattern for the likelihood that Millennials are willing to volunteer in their communities. Compared to older adults, Millennials in South Africa, Chile, and Mexico place more importance on local volunteerism. Conversely, non-Millennials in the United States and Australia rate this activity as being more important in comparison to the younger generation.

We also found that Millennials are just as likely as, if not more likely than older adults to engage with political organizations and participate in problem-solving activities at the local level. In six of the eight countries, Millennials expressed greater interest than non-Millennials in this type of engagement. These differences were more pronounced in the United Kingdom, Australia, and New Zealand. This result is yet another example of how less conventional forms of political participation have particular appeal for the Millennial Generation.

Finally, and perhaps most important, we showed that Millennials are even more confident than older generations in their ability to serve in leadership positions in politics. In the United States, the United Kingdom, South Africa, and New Zealand, Millennials report feeling more qualified, while in Australia, Chile, and South Korea, they feel slightly less qualified, compared to non-Millennials. There was no difference between Millennials and older cohorts in Mexico. As older citizens retire from public service, this result suggests, there may not be a leadership gap and there is a pool of younger citizens potentially ready to be at the head of local government. Though Millennials may have relative distaste for voting, they seem to be open to serving in local office. This finding is an example of how the line between "duty-based" and "active" citizenship for the Millennial Generation may not be absolute. Based on our overarching results in this and other chapters, Millennials are certainly more likely to prefer being active. However, if they are willing to run for and serve in local public office (a presumed extension of feeling qualified for the job), there may be less distance between the two, and therefore an opportunity for a fertile middle ground.

Conclusion: Millennials—a Generation Poised to Lead in Global Governance?

On August 30, 2021, the United States completed its withdrawal of armed forces from Afghanistan. This act marked the end of a twenty-year war, the longest in American history. Most Americans supported the withdrawal (although not necessarily how it was carried out; Van Green and Doherty 2021) and saw it as an end to an unsuccessful foreign policy mission. However, for the rest of the world it may have represented a change in perspective about both the hard and soft global power of the United States from the one projected fifty years ago. The potential waning of U.S. soft power and perhaps the greater hesitation to use hard power may be an inflection point and presents an important opportunity to think about how global governance can take shape over the next thirty years. There is little doubt that the Millennial Generation will have a crucial say in how this comes about.

In this book, we have advanced the importance of understanding group-based identities from a generational perspective. This identity type has been largely ignored, particularly in the comparative literature. The Millennial Generation, those adults who are now in their mid twenties to early forties, are poised to make up a large portion of political, economic, and social leaders and will soon decide the future of both national and international governance. As our results demonstrate, Millennials, by many measures, are global citizens, and politically they behave much more uniformly as a group compared to older adults. We argue that this has important implications for how critical and worldwide issues will be addressed in the future. There is likely no better test of this than with the issue of climate change. Millennials consider climate change to be the world's most serious issue (Chow 2017), and this concern grows when individuals are encouraged to think about how it might impact the world in the future (Yeager et al. 2011). In November 2021, U.S. President Joe Biden joined other world leaders in Glasgow for the United Nations Climate Change Conference (known as COP26) to forge a new agreement to limit global warming. Biden, a member of the Silent Generation, went to Glasgow to display the U.S. commitment to and leadership in the global climate crisis. But despite this public display of support for climate action, the United States has remained unwilling or unable to meet its obligations. U.S. efforts to address climate change are marred by internal country conflicts, where there is not a sufficient consensus on the effects of human behavior on global warming to force substantial remedial action. In fact, in 2017 President Donald Trump pulled the United States out of the Paris Agreement—the only country out of two hundred signatories to make such a move (Ross and Rouse 2020).

With little agreement or action on such an important issue as climate change, long-term challenges arising from a global pandemic, and U.S. power and leadership waning or lacking on the global stage, it seems increasingly unlikely that the world's biggest problems can be solved purely by conventional means of political engagement (e.g., voting) by the world's younger generations. Rather, it may take a more nonconventional and engaged approach that can arise only in a group whose identity is grounded in norms, values, and experiences forged by a sense of global citizenship and the innate ability to leverage technology to bring about both unity and change. An important question will be how quickly older adults are willing to pass the leadership baton to Millennials or at least step out of the way and allow this generation to embrace the grand challenges they may not have created but will fully inherit.

Global Millennial Survey Questionnaire

Q1. In terms of what's important about you, how much do you identify with each of the following on the scale presented?

[RANDOMIZE ROWS]	Not at all 1	2	3	4	5	6	7	8	9	Very Strongly 10
Q1a. A citizen of <COUNTRY>	1	2	3	4	5	6	7	8	9	10
Q1b. A citizen of the world	1	2	3	4	5	6	7	8	9	10
Q1c. A follower of your religious faith	1	2	3	4	5	6	7	8	9	10
Q1d. A member of your race	1	2	3	4	5	6	7	8	9	10
Q1e. A member of your generation or age group	1	2	3	4	5	6	7	8	9	10
Q1f. Part of your ethnic group	1	2	3	4	5	6	7	8	9	10
Q1g. Your gender	1	2	3	4	5	6	7	8	9	10
Q1h. Your class or socioeconomic status	1	2	3	4	5	6	7	8	9	10

120 GLOBAL MILLENNIAL SURVEY QUESTIONNAIRE

Q2: Which one of these identities is **most** important to you today? Please select one.

1. A citizen of <COUNTRY>
2. A citizen of the world
3. A follower of your religious faith
4. A member of your race
5. A member of your generation or age group
6. Part of your ethnic group
7. Your gender
8. Your class or economic status

Q3: Please rank the following reasons you are most likely to support a leader or someone seeking to be a leader in your country?

1. She/he says what is on his/her mind
2. He/she has a lot of experience
3. She/he represents the issues I care about
4. He/she is most likely to bring about change
5. She/he cares about people like me
6. Other

Q4: How closely do you follow politics?

1. Not at all
2. Not very closely
3. Somewhat closely
4. Very closely

GLOBAL MILLENNIAL SURVEY QUESTIONNAIRE 121

Q5: Please rank your sources for political information?

1. The internet
2. Social media
3. Television
4. Radio
5. Newspaper/magazine (in print)
6. Other

Q6: How difficult do you feel it is to get accurate political information in general?

1. Not difficult at all
2. Not very difficult
3. Somewhat difficult
4. Very difficult

Q7: How difficult do you feel it is to get accurate political information from the internet or social media?

1. Not difficult at all
2. Not very difficult
3. Somewhat difficult
4. Very difficult

122 GLOBAL MILLENNIAL SURVEY QUESTIONNAIRE

For each pair of statements below, please use the scale to indicate where your opinion falls with regard to the two statements.

Q8.	Cutting government spending is the only way to improve our economic outlook 1	2	3	4	More government spending is needed to alleviate the economic hardships Americans are suffering 5
Q9.	The government should provide national health insurance that everyone pays into and has ac- cess to when going to their doctor 1	2	3	4	The government should stay out of all healthcare insurance decisions, and let those who want it to buy it themselves or get it through their employer 5
Q10.	1 <COUNTRY SPECIFIC>	2	3	4	5 <COUNTRY SPECIFIC>
Q11.	1 <COUNTRY SPECIFIC>	2	3	4	5 <COUNTRY SPECIFIC>
Q12.	1 <COUNTRY SPECIFIC>	2	3	4	5 <COUNTRY SPECIFIC>
Q13.	Diplomatic methods of negotiations or sanctions is best way to address international threats 1	2	3	4	Armed/militarized ac- tion or force is best way to address international threats 5

GLOBAL MILLENNIAL SURVEY QUESTIONNAIRE   123

Q14: For each of the following forms of political and social actions, please indicate whether or not you have participated recently; in the distant past; never, but you would consider it; or never, and you would never consider engaging in the political or social action:

A. Vote in an election

  1. I have never done this, and would never do it
  2. I have never done this, but I might do it
  3. I have done this, but it was over a year ago
  4. I have done this within the past year

B. Be a member of a political party

  1. I have never done this, and would never do it
  2. I have never done this, but I might do it
  3. I have done this, but it was over a year ago
  4. I have done this within the past year

C. Sign a petition

  1. I have never done this, and would never do it
  2. I have never done this, but I might do it
  3. I have done this, but it was over a year ago
  4. I have done this within the past year

D. Boycott products, or deliberately buy products, for political or ethical reasons

  1. I have never done this, and would never do it
  2. I have never done this, but I might do it
  3. I have done this, but it was over a year ago
  4. I have done this within the past year

124 GLOBAL MILLENNIAL SURVEY QUESTIONNAIRE

E. Take part in a demonstration

1. I have never done this, and would never do it
2. I have never done this, but I might do it
3. I have done this, but it was over a year ago
4. I have done this within the past year

F. Attend a political meeting or rally

1. I have never done this, and would never do it
2. I have never done this, but I might do it
3. I have done this, but it was over a year ago
4. I have done this within the past year

G. Contact a politician or public official to express your views

1. I have never done this, and would never do it
2. I have never done this, but I might do it
3. I have done this, but it was over a year ago
4. I have done this within the past year

H. Donate money or raise funds for a political activity

1. I have never done this, and would never do it
2. I have never done this, but I might do it
3. I have done this, but it was over a year ago
4. I have done this within the past year

I. Participate in an internet forum or discussion group to discuss political issues

1. I have never done this, and would never do it
2. I have never done this, but I might do it

3. I have done this, but it was over a year ago
4. I have done this within the past year

J. Attend a religious service

1. I have never done this, and would never do it
2. I have never done this, but I might do it
3. I have done this, but it was over a year ago
4. I have done this within the past year

K. Volunteer to help those in need in your community

1. I have never done this, and would never do it
2. I have never done this, but I might do it
3. I have done this, but it was over a year ago
4. I have done this within the past year

126 GLOBAL MILLENNIAL SURVEY QUESTIONNAIRE

Q15. In terms of what's important to you, how do you rate the effectiveness of each of the following on the scale presented?

[RANDOMIZE ROWS; GROUP ITEMS A + B, C + D, E + F]	Not at all	2	3	4	5	6	7	8	9	Very Important
Q15a Voting in local elections	1	2	3	4	5	6	7	8	9	10
Q15b. Voting in national elections	1	2	3	4	5	6	7	8	9	10
Q15c. Engaging in political activities aimed at changing local conditions	1	2	3	4	5	6	7	8	9	10
Q15d. Engaging in political activities aimed at changing national conditions	1	2	3	4	5	6	7	8	9	10
Q15e. Joining a local political organization	1	2	3	4	5	6	7	8	9	10
Q15f. Joining a national political organization	1	2	3	4	5	6	7	8	9	10

GLOBAL MILLENNIAL SURVEY QUESTIONNAIRE   127

Q16. In terms of what's important about you, how much do you agree with each of the following on the scale presented?

[RANDOMIZE ROWS]	Not at all	2	3	4	5	6	7	8	9	Very Strongly
Q16a. Government officials care about the opinions of people like me	1	2	3	4	5	6	7	8	9	10
Q16b. Parties are only interested in my vote, not my opinion	1	2	3	4	5	6	7	8	9	10
Q16c. People like me have no influence on politics	1	2	3	4	5	6	7	8	9	10
Q16d. Because so many people vote, my vote does not matter	1	2	3	4	5	6	7	8	9	10
Q16e. Public officials quickly lose contact with citizens	1	2	3	4	5	6	7	8	9	10
Q16f. I feel that I could do as good a job in public office as most people	1	2	3	4	5	6	7	8	9	10
Q16g. I feel that I have a pretty good understanding of the important political issues facing <COUNTRY>	1	2	3	4	5	6	7	8	9	10

Notes

Chapter 1

1. According to the World Economic Forum 2021.

Chapter 2

1. Different organizations have defined the Millennial Generation using different birth years, but 1981–1996 has become widely accepted and is used by the Pew Research Center. Because we collected our data prior to this consensus, we look at 1983–2000, which is the same range used by the U.S. Public Interest Research Group and very similar to the 1982–2000 range used previously by the U.S. Census.
2. The Global Web Index worldwide survey of social media use is cited in World Economic Forum 2019.
3. Based on the United Nations Human Development Index (Conceição 2020), South Africa scores a 0.705. For comparison, Mexico is the next lowest country in our dataset at 0.767, while countries like Japan and the United States are 0.915 and 0.920, respectively.

Chapter 3

1. Low levels of support for diplomacy among those over the age of thirty-five in the United States are primarily responsible for the greater range among the older age cohort.

Chapter 4

1. All indicators were considered as a yes/no dummy coded variable.

Works Cited

Abramson, Paul R., and John H. Aldrich. 1982. "The Decline of Electoral Participation in America." *American Political Science Review* 76(3): 502–521. https://doi.org/10.2307/1963728.

Adkins, Amy. n.d. "Millennials: The Job-Hopping Generation." Gallup. https://www.gallup.com/workplace/231587/millennials-job-hopping-generation.aspx.

Ajzen, Icek. 1991. "The Theory of Planned Behavior." *Organizational Behavior and Human Decision Processes* 50(2): 179–211. https://doi.org/10.1016/0749-5978(91)90020-T.

Akumina. 2019. "2019 Millennial Manager Survey." June 6. https://letsgo.akumina.com/WC-2019-06-05MillennialManagerSurveyReport_LP-Registration.html.

Almond, Gabriel A., and Sidney Verba. 1963. *The Civic Culture: Political Attitudes and Democracy in Five Nations.* Princeton University Press. https://www.jstor.org/stable/j.ctt183pnr2.

Alwin, Duane F., and Jon A. Krosnick. 1991. "Aging, Cohorts, and the Stability of Sociopolitical Orientations over the Life Span." *American Journal of Sociology* 97(1): 169–195.

ANES. 2014. "User's Guide and Codebook for the ANES 2012 Time Series Study." The University of Michigan and Stanford University.

Antunovic, Dunja, Patrick Parsons, and Tanner R. Cooke. 2018. "'Checking' and Googling: Stages of News Consumption among Young Adults." *Journalism* 19(5): 632–648.

Atkeson, Lonna Rae. 2003. "Not All Cues Are Created Equal: The Conditional Impact of Female Candidates on Political Engagement." *Journal of Politics* 65(4): 1040–1061.

Baker, Kendall L. 1973. "Political Participation, Political Efficacy, and Socialization in Germany." *Comparative Politics* 6(1): 73–98. https://doi.org/10.2307/421346.

Bandura, Albert. 1977. "Self-Efficacy: Toward a Unifying Theory of Behavioral Change." *Psychological Review* 84(2): 191–215. https://doi.org/10.1037/0033-295X.84.2.191.

Bartels, Larry M., and Simon Jackman. 2014. "A Generational Model of Political Learning." *Electoral Studies* 33: 7–18.

Beaumont, Elizabeth. 2010. "Political Agency and Empowerment: Pathways for Developing a Sense of Political Efficacy in Young Adults." In *Handbook*

132 WORKS CITED

of Research on Civic Engagement in Youth, edited by L. R. Sherrod, J. Torney-Purta, and C. A. Flanagan, 525–558. Hoboken, New Jersey: Wiley-Blackwell. https://doi.org/10.1002/9780470767603.ch20.

Beck, Paul A., and M. Kent Jennings. 1982. "Pathways to Participation." *American Political Science Review* 76(1): 94–108.

Benetsky, Charlynn, A. Burd, and Melanie A. Rapino. 2015. *Young Adult Migration: 2007–2009 to 2010–2012.* Washington, DC: United States Census Bureau.

Bennett, Stephen E., Richard S. Flickinger, and Staci L. Rhine. 2000. "Political Talk Over Here, Over There, Over Time." *British Journal of Political Science* 30(1): 99–119. https://doi.org/10.1017/S0007123400000053.

Berinsky, Adam J. 2017. "Rumors and Health Care Reform: Experiments in Political Misinformation." *British Journal of Political Science* 47(2): 241–262.

Best, Samuel J., and Brian S. Krueger. 2005. "Analyzing the Representativeness of Internet Political Participation." *Political Behavior* 27(2): 183–216. https://doi.org/10.1007/s11109-005-3242-y.

Bolzendahl, Catherine, and Hilde Coffé. 2009. "Citizenship beyond Politics: The Importance of Political, Civil and Social Rights and Responsibilities among Women and Men." *The British Journal of Sociology* 60(4): 763–791. https://doi.org/10.1111/j.1468-4446.2009.01274.x.

Bolzendahl, Catherine, and Hilde Coffé. 2013. "Are 'Good' Citizens 'Good' Participants? Testing Citizenship Norms and Political Participation across 25 Nations." *Political Studies* 61(suppl 1): 45–65. https://doi.org/10.1111/1467-9248.12010.

Brady, Henry E., Sidney Verba, and Kay Lehman Schlozman. 1995. "Beyond SES: A Resource Model of Political Participation." *American Political Science Review* 89(2): 271–294. https://doi.org/10.2307/2082425.

Brannen, Samuel J., Christian S. Haig, and Katherine Schmidt. 2020. "The Age of Mass Protest." The Age of Mass Protests. Center for Strategic and International Studies (CSIS). https://www.jstor.org/stable/resrep22600.1.

Braungart, Richard, and Margaret M. Braungart. 1986. "Life Course and Generational Politics." *Annual Review of Sociology* 12: 205–231.

Brown, Heather, Emily Guskin, and Amy Mitchell. 2012. "The Role of Social Media in the Arab Uprisings." Pew Research Center, November 28. https://www.journalism.org/2012/11/28/role-social-media-arab-uprisings/.

Campbell, Angus, Gerald Gurin, and Warren Edward Miller. 1954. *The Voter Decides.* Evanston, IL: Row, Peterson, and Co.

Campbell, David E. 2006. *Why We Vote: How Schools and Communities Shape Our Civic Life.* Princeton, NJ: Princeton University Press.

Campbell, David E. 2009. "Civic Engagement and Education: An Empirical Test of the Sorting Model." *American Journal of Political Science* 53(4): 771–786.

WORKS CITED   133

Campbell, David E., and Christina Wolbrecht. 2006. "See Jane Run: Women Politicians as Role Models for Adolescents." *Journal of Politics* 68(2): 233–247.

Castells, Manuel 2015. *Networks of Outrage and Hope: Social Movements in the Internet Age*. Wiley.

Center for American Women and Politics. 2019. "Women in Elective Office 2019." https://www.cawp.rutgers.edu/women-elective-office-2019.

Chayinska, Maria, Daniel Miranda, and Roberto González. 2021. "A Longitudinal Study of the Bidirectional Causal Relationships between Online Political Participation and Offline Collective Action." *Computers in Human Behavior* 121: 1–12. https://doi.org/10.1016/j.chb.2021.106810.

Chipkin, Ivor, and Annie Leatt. 2011. "Religion and Revival in Post-Apartheid South Africa." *Religion & Society* 62: 39–46.

Chow, Lorraine. 2017. "Millennials: Climate Change Is World's Biggest Problem." *EcoWatch*, September 7. https://www.ecowatch.com/millennials-climate-change-2482557556.html#toggle-gdpr.

Citrin, Jack, Beth Reingold, and Donald P. Green. 1990. "American Identity and the Politics of Ethnic Change." *Journal of Politics* 52(4): 1124–1154.

CNBC. 2019. "Social Media Has Become a Battleground in Hong Kong's Protests." August 15. https://www.cnbc.com/2019/08/16/social-media-has-become-a-battleground-in-hong-kongs-protests.html.

Coffé, Hilde, and Tanja van der Lippe. 2010. "Citizenship Norms in Eastern Europe." *Social Indicators Research* 96(3): 479–496. https://doi.org/10.1007/s11205-009-9488-8.

Cole, Juan. 2014. *The New Arabs: How the Millennial Generation Is Changing the Middle East*. New York: Simon & Schuster.

Conceição, Pedro. 2020. "The Next Frontier: Human Development and the Anthropocene." United Nations Human Development Programme. New York, NY.

Craig, Stephen C., Richard G. Niemi, and Glenn E. Silver. 1990. "Political Efficacy and Trust: A Report on the NES Pilot Study Items." *Political Behavior* 12(3): 289–314. https://doi.org/10.1007/BF00992337.

Crocker, Jennifer, and Brenda Major. 1989. "Social Stigma and Self-Esteem: The Self-Protective Properties of Stigma." *Psychological Review* 96(4): 608–630.

Dalton, Russell J. 2015. *The Good Citizen; How a Younger Generation Is Reshaping American Politics*, 2nd edition. Los Angeles, CA: CQ Press.

DeHart-Davis, Leisha, Justin Marlowe, and Sanjay K. Pandey. 2006. "Gender Dimensions of Public Service Motivation." *Public Administration Review* 66: 873–887.

Della Porta, Donatella. 2013. *Can Democracy Be Saved: Participation, Deliberation and Social Movements*, 1st edition. Cambridge, UK: Polity.

Delli Carpini, Michael X., and Scott Keeter. 1996. *What Americans Know about Politics and Why It Matters*. New Haven, CT: Yale University Press.

134 WORKS CITED

Dinas, Elias. 2013. "Opening 'Openness to Change': Political Events and the Increased Sensitivity of Young Adults." *Political Research Quarterly* 66(4): 868–882.

Dubois, Elizabeth, and Grant Blank. 2018. "The Echo Chamber Is Overstated: The Moderating Effect of Political Interest and Diverse Media." *Information Communication and Society* 21(5): 729–745.

Easton, David, and Jack Dennis. 1967. "The Child's Acquisition of Regime Norms: Political Efficacy." *The American Political Science Review* 61(1): 25–38. https://doi.org/10.2307/1953873.

Easton, David, and Jack Dennis. 1969. *Children in the Political System: Origins of Political Legitimacy.* New York: McGraw-Hill.

Ekman, Joakim, and Erik Amnå. 2012. "Political Participation and Civic Engagement: Towards a New Typology." *Human Affairs* 22(3): 283–300. https://doi.org/10.2478/s13374-012-0024-1.

Erickson, Robert S., and Laura Stoker. 2011. "Caught in the Draft: The Effects of Vietnam Draft Lottery Status on Political Attitudes." *American Political Science Review* 105(2): 221–237.

Erkulwater, Juliet. 2012. "Political Participation over the Life Cycle." In *The Unheavenly Chorus: Unequal Political Voice and the Broken Promise of American Democracy,* edited by Kay L. Schlozman, Sidney Verba, and Henry E. Brady, 199–231. Princeton, NJ: Princeton University Press.

ESS Round 6. 2012. "European Social Survey Round 6 DataData file edition 2.0." Norwegian Social Science Data Services, Norway: Data Archive and distributor of ESS data.

Eveland Jr, William P., and Dietram A. Scheufele. 2000. "Connecting News Media Use with Gaps in Knowledge and Participation." *Political Communication* 17(3): 215–237. https://doi.org/10.1080/105846000414250.

Ferri-Reed, Jan. 2013. "Leading a Multi-Generational Workforce—Quality, Conflict, and Communication across the Generations." *Journal for Quality and Participation* 35(4): 12–14.

Finkel, Steven E. 1985. "Reciprocal Effects of Participation and Political Efficacy: A Panel Analysis." *American Journal of Political Science* 29(4): 891–913. https://doi.org/10.2307/2111186.

Flaxman, Seth, Sharad Goel, and Justin M. Rao. 2016. "Filter Bubbles, Echo Chambers, and Online News Consumption." *Public Opinion Quarterly* 80(SI-1): 298–320.

Fox, Richard L. and Jennifer L. Lawless. 2014. "Uncovering the Origins of the Gender Gap in Political Ambition." *American Political Science Review* 108(3): 499–519.

Frey, William H. 2018. "The Millennial Generation: A Demographic Bridge to America's Diverse Future." Report. Washington, DC: Brookings Institute.

Gainous, Jason, Adam David Marlowe, and Kevin M. Wagner. 2013. "Traditional Cleavages or a New World: Does Online Social Networking

WORKS CITED 135

Bridge the Political Participation Divide?" *International Journal of Politics, Culture, and Society* 26(2): 145–158. https://doi.org/10.1007/s10 767-013-9130-2.

Gallup. 2017. "How Millennials Want to Work and Live." https://www.gallup.com/workplace/238073/millennials-work-live.aspx.

García-Albacete, Gema M. 2014. *Young People's Political Participation in Western Europe: Continuity or Generational Change?* Palgrave Macmillan. https://doi.org/10.1057/9781137341310.

Gerber, Alan, and Donald Green. 1999. "Misperceptions about Perceptual Bias." *Annual Review of Political Science* 2: 189–210.

Gerber, Alan S., Donald P. Green, and Ron Shachar. 2003. "Voting May Be Habit-Forming: Evidence from a Randomized Field Experiment." *American Journal of Political Science* 47(3): 540–550. https://doi.org/10.1111/1540-5907.00038.

Gilens, Martin. 2012. *Affluence and Influence: Economic Inequality and Political Power in America.* Princeton University Press. https://doi.org/10.2307/j.ctt7s1jn.

Glenn, Norval D., and Michael Grimes. 1968. "Aging, Voting, and Political Interest." *American Sociological Review* 33(4): 563–575. https://doi.org/10.2307/2092441.

González, Roberto, Belén Alvarez, Jorge Manzi, Micaela Varela, Cristián Frigolett, Andrew G. Livingstone, Winnifred Louis et al. 2021. "The Role of Family in the Intergenerational Transmission of Collective Action." *Social Psychological and Personality Science* 12(6): 856–867. https://doi.org/10.1177/1948550620949378.

Ha, Louisa, Ying Xu, Chen Yang, Fang Wang, Liu Yang, Mohammad Abuljadail, Xiao Hu, Weiwei Jiang, and Itay Gabay. 2008. "Decline in News Content Engagement or News Medium Engagement? A Longitudinal Analysis of News Engagement since the Rise of Social and Mobile Media 2009–2012." *Journalism* 19(5): 718–739.

Hadjar, Andreas, and Rolf Becker. 2007. "Unkonventionelle Politische Partizipation Im Zeitverlauf." *KZfSS Kölner Zeitschrift für Soziologie und Sozialpsychologie* 59(3): 410–439. https://doi.org/10.1007/s11 577-007-0055-5.

Hayes, Bernadette C., and Clive S. Bean. 1993. "Political Efficacy: A Comparative Study of the United States, West Germany, Great Britain and Australia." *European Journal of Political Research* 23(3): 261–280. https://doi.org/10.1111/j.1475-6765.1993.tb00359.x.

Hellevik, Ottar. 2002. "Age Differences in Value Orientation—Life Cycle or Cohort Effects?" *International Journal of Public Opinion Research* 14(3): 286–302.

Hello, Evelyn, Peer Scheepers, Ad Vermulst, and Jan R. M. Gerris. 2004. "Association between Educational Attainment and Ethnic Distance in

136 WORKS CITED

Young Adults: Socialization by Schools or Parents?" *Acta Sociologica* 47: 253–275.

Henderson, Michael. 2014. "Issue Publics, Campaigns, and Political Knowledge." *Political Behavior* 36: 631–657.

Highton, Benjamin, and Raymond E. Wolfinger. 2001. "The First Seven Years of the Political Life Cycle." *American Journal of Political Science* 45(1): 202–209. https://doi.org/10.2307/2669367.

Holbein, John B., and D. Sunshine Hillygus. 2020. *Making Young Voters: Converting Civic Attitudes into Civic Action.* Cambridge: Cambridge University Press. https://doi.org/10.1017/9781108770446.

Hopkins, Daniel J., John Sides, and Jack Citrin. 2019. "The Muted Consequences of Correct Information about Immigration." *Journal of Politics* 81(1): 315–320.

Hopper, Paul. 2007. *Understanding Cultural Globalization.* Cambridge, UK: Polity.

Howe, Neil. 2014. "The Silent Generation, 'The Lucky Few.'" *Forbes,* August 13. https://www.forbes.com/sites/neilhowe/2014/08/13/the-silent-generation-the-lucky-few-part-3-of-7/#47e6e25e2c63.

Howe, Neil, and William Strauss. 2000. *Millennials Rising: The Next Great Generation.* New York: Vintage.

Huddy, Leonie. 2001. "From Social to Political Identity: A Critical Examination of Social Identity Theory." *Political Psychology* 22: 127–156.

IDEA. 2016. "Voter Turnout Trends around the World." https://www.idea.int/publications/catalogue/voter-turnout-trends-around-world.

Iyengar, Shanto. 1980. "Subjective Political Efficacy as a Measure of Diffuse Support." *Public Opinion Quarterly* 44(2): 249–256. https://doi.org/10.1086/268589.

Jacobson, Susan, Eunyoung Myung, and Steven L. Johnson. 2016. "Open Media or Echo Chamber: The Use of Links in Audience Discussions on the Facebook Pages of Partisan News Organizations." *Information Communication & Society* 19(7): 875–891.

Jardina, Ashley. 2019. *White Identity Politics.* New York: Cambridge University Press.

Jennings, M. Kent. 2015. "The Dynamics of Good Citizenship Norms." In *Citizenship and Democracy in an Era of Crisis,* edited by Thomas Poguntke, Sigrid Rossteutscher, Rüdiger Schmitt-Beck and Sonja Zmerli, 93–111. London: Routledge. https://doi.org/10.4324/9781315750248.

Jennings, M. Kent, and Richard G. Niemi. 1968. "The Transmission of Political Values from Parent to Child." *American Political Science Review* 62(1): 169–184.

Jennings, M. Kent, and Richard G. Niemi. 1974. *Political Character of Adolescence: The Influence of Families and Schools.* Princeton University Press. https://www.jstor.org/stable/j.ctt13x0sjz.

WORKS CITED   137

Jennings, M. Kent, and Richard G. Niemi. 1981. *Generations and Politics: A Panel Study of Young Adults and Their Parents*. Princeton, NJ: Princeton University Press.

Kavanagh, Jennifer, William Marcellino, Jonathan S. Blake, Shawn Smith, Steven Davenport, and Mahlet G. Tebeka. 2019. "News in a Digital Age: Comparing the Presentation of News Information over Time and across Media Platforms." Report. Santa Monica, CA: RAND. https://www.rand.org/pubs/research_reports/RR2960.html.

Kim, Sangmook. 2016. "Job Characteristics, Public Service Motivation, and Work Performance in Korea." *Gestion et Management Public* 5: 7–24.

Kinder, Donald R., and David O. Sears. 1985. "Public Opinion and Political Action." In *Handbook of Social Psychology,* 3rd ed., edited by G. Lindzey and E. Aronson, vol. 2, 659–741. New York: Random House.

Koestner, Richard, and Gaëtan F. Losier. 2002. "Distinguishing Three Ways of Being Highly Motivated: A Closer Look at Introjection, Identification, and Intrinsic Motivation." In *Handbook of Self-Determination Research*, edited by Edward L. Deci and Richard M. Ryan, 101–121. Rochester, NY: University of Rochester Press.

Kohut, Andy. 2013. "Pew Surveys of Audience Habits Suggest Perilous Future for News." *Poynter*. https://www.poynter.org/newsletters/2013/pew-surv eys-of-audience-habits-suggest-perilous-future-for-news/

Korean Times. 2020. "Activists to Hold Rally Supporting Black Lives Matter Movement in Seoul." June 5. https://www.koreatimes.co.kr/www/nation/2020/06/177_290728.html.

Kotzé, Hennie, and Reinet Loubser. 2017. "Religiosity in South Africa: Trends among the Public and Elites." *Scriptura: Journal for Biblical, Theological and Contextual Hermeneutics* 116(1): 1–12.

Kuklinski, James H., Paul J. Quirk, Jennifer Jerit, and Robert F. Rich. 2001. "The Political Environment and Citizen Competence." *American Journal of Political Science* 45(2): 410–424.

Kuklinski, James H., Paul J. Quirk, Jennifer Jerit, Daniel Schwieder, and Robert F. Rich. 2000. "Misinformation and the Currency of Democratic Citizenship." *Journal of Politics* 62(3): 790–816.

Langton, Kenneth P. 1967. "Peer Group and School and the Political Socialization Process." *American Political Science Review* 61(3): 751–758.

Lazarus, Richard S. 1991. *Emotion and Adaptation*. New York: Oxford University Press.

Lazer, David M. J., Matthew Baum, Yochai Benkler, Adam J. Berinsky, Kelly M. Greenhill, Filippo Menczer, Miriam J. Metzger, Brendan Nyhan, Gordon Pennycook, David Rothschild, Michael Schudson, Steven A. Sloman, Cass R. Sunstein, Emily A. Thorson, Duncan J. Watts, and Jonathan L. Zittrain. 2018. "The Science of Fake News." *Science* 359(6380): 1094–1096.

138   WORKS CITED

Lerner, Michele. 2019. "Millennials Now Represent the Largest Cohort of Home Buyers. Here's What They Are Looking For." *Washington Post*. December 12.

Levy, Brett L. M., and Thomas Akiva. 2019. "Motivating Political Participation Among Youth: An Analysis of Factors Related to Adolescents' Political Engagement." *Political Psychology* 40(5): 1039–1055. https://doi.org/10.1111/pops.12578.

Lewandowsky, Stephen, Ullrich K. H. Ecker, and John Cook. 2017 "Beyond Misinformation: Understanding and Coping with the 'Post-Truth' Era." *Journal of Applied Research in Memory and Cognition* 6(4): 353–369.

Livingston, Gretchen. 2018. "More Than a Million Millennials Are Becoming Moms Each Year." Pew Research Report, May 4. https://www.pewresearch.org/fact-tank/2018/05/04/more-than-a-million-millennials-are-becoming-moms-each-year/.

Loader, Brian D., and Dan Mercea. 2011. "Networking Democracy? Social Media Innovations and Participatory Politics." *Information, Communication & Society* 14(6): 757–769.

Lönnqvist, Jan-Erik and Juha V. A. Itkonen. 2016. "Homogeneity of Personal Values and Personality Traits in Facebook Social Networks." *Journal of Research in Personality* 60: 24–35.

Lupia, Arthur, and Tasha S. Philpot. 2005. "Views from Inside the Net: How Websites Affect Young Adults' Political Interest." *The Journal of Politics* 67(4): 1122–1142. https://doi.org/10.1111/j.1468-2508.2005.00353.x.

Marx, Paul, and Christoph Nguyen. 2016. "Are the Unemployed Less Politically Involved? A Comparative Study of Internal Political Efficacy." *European Sociological Review* 32(5): 634–648. https://doi.org/10.1093/esr/jcw020.

Mason, Lilliana. 2018. *Uncivil Agreement: How Politics Became Our Identity*. Chicago: University of Chicago Press.

Masullo Chen, Gina, Yee Man Margaret Ng, Martin J. Riedl, and Victoria Y. Chen. 2020. "Exploring How Online Political Quizzes Boost Interest in Politics, Political News, and Political Engagement." *Journal of Information Technology & Politics* 17(1): 33–47. https://doi.org/10.1080/19331681.2019.1680475.

Milbrath, Lester W., and Madan Lal Goel. 1977. *Political Participation: How and Why Do People Get Involved in Politics?* Rand McNally College Pub. Co.

Miranda, Daniel, Juan Carlos Castillo, and Andrés Sandoval-Hernandez. 2020. "Young Citizens Participation: Empirical Testing of a Conceptual Model." *Youth & Society* 52(2): 251–271. https://doi.org/10.1177/0044118X17741024.

Mutz, Diana. 2006. *Hearing the Other Side*. Cambridge: Cambridge University Press.

Nelson, Jacob L., and James G. Webster. 2017. "The Myth of Partisan Selective Exposure: A Portrait of the Online Political News Audience." *Social Media and Society* 3(3).

WORKS CITED 139

Neundorf, Anja, and Kaat Smets. 2017. "Political Socialization and the Making of Citizens." *Oxford Handbooks Online*. February 6. https://doi.org/10.1093/oxfordhb/9780199935307.013.98.

Neundorf, Anja, Richard G. Niemi, and Kaat Smets. 2016. "The Compensation Effect of Civic Education on Political Engagement: How Civics Classes Make Up For Missing Parental Socialization." *Political Behavior* 38(4): 921–949.

Newman, Nic, Richard Fletcher, Antonis Kalogeropoulos, and Rasmus Kleis Nielsen. 2019. "Reuters Institute Digital News Report." Reuters Institute and the University of Oxford. https://www.digitalnewsreport.org/survey/2019/overview-key-findings-2019/.

New York Times. 2018. "South Korea Declares War on 'Fake News,' Worrying Government Critics." October 2.

Nie, Norman H., Jane Junn, and Kenneth Stehlik-Barry. 1996. *Education and Democratic Citizenship in America*. Chicago: University of Chicago Press.

Niemi, Richard G., and Barbara I. Sobieszek, 1977. "Political Socialization." *Annual Review of Sociology* 3: 209–233.

Norris, Pippa. 2011. *Democratic Deficit: Critical Citizens Revisited*. Cambridge University Press. https://doi.org/10.1017/CBO9780511973383.

Norris, Pippa, and Ronald Inglehart. 2004. *Sacred and Secular: Religion and Politics Worldwide*. New York: Cambridge University Press.

Nussbaum, Martha C. 1996. "Patriotism and Cosmopolitanism." In *For Love of Country?*, edited by Martha Nussbaum and Joshua Cohen. Boston: Beacon Press, 3–17.

Nussbaum, Martha C. 2008. "Toward a Globally Sensitive Patriotism." *Daedalus* 137(3): 78–93.

Nwanevu, Osita. 2020. "The Rise of the Permanent Protest." *The New Republic*, 1 de enero de 2020. https://newrepublic.com/article/155893/rise-permanent-protest-decade-from-hell.

Nyhan, Brendan, Ethan Porter, Jason Reifler, and Thomas J. Wood. 2019. "Taking Corrections Literally but Not Seriously? The Effects of Information on Factual Beliefs and Candidate Favorability." *Political Behavior* 42: 939–960.

Nyhan, Brendan, and Jason Reifler. 2010. "When Corrections Fail: The Persistence of Political Misperceptions." *Political Behavior* 32(2): 303–330.

Nyhan, Brendan, Jason Reifler, and Peter A. Ubel. 2013. "The Hazards of Correcting Myths about Health Care Reform." *Medical Care* 51(2): 127–132.

Papastephanou, Marianna. 2013. "Cosmopolitanism Discarded: Martha Nussbaum's Patriotic Education and the Inward-Outward Distinction." *Ethics and Education* 8(2): 166–178.

Pariser, Eli. 2011. *The Filter Bubble: How the New Personalized Web Is Changing What We Read and How We Think*. London: Penguin Press.

Perry, James L., and Lois Recascino Wise. 1990. "The Motivational Bases of Public Service." *Public Administration Review* 50(3): 367–373.

140 WORKS CITED

Pew Forum on Religion and Public Life. "Religion and Public Life Survey, 2009. *The Pew Research Center for the People and the Press*. https://www.thea rda.com/Archive/Files/Descriptions/RELPUB09.asp.

Pew Research Center. 2010. "For Millennials, Parenthood Trumps Marriage." https://www.pewresearch.org/social-trends/2011/03/09/for-millennials-parenthood-trumps-marriage/.

Pew Research Center. 2012. "The Role of Social Media in the Arab Uprisings." https://www.pewresearch.org/journalism/2012/11/28/role-social-media-arab-uprisings/.

Pew Research Center. 2014a. "Global Attitudes Survey." Spring. https://www.pewresearch.org/global/dataset/2014-spring-global-attitudes/.

Pew Research Center. 2014b. "Millennials in Adulthood: Detached from Institutions, Networked with Friends." https://www.pewresearch.org/soc ial-trends/2014/03/07/millennials-in-adulthood/.

Pew Research Center. 2018. "Teens, Social Media and Technology 2018." https://www.pewresearch.org/internet/2018/05/31/teens-social-media-tec hnology-2018/.

Pew Research Center. 2019. "Social Media Fact Sheet." https://www.pewresea rch.org/internet/fact-sheet/social-media/.

Pison, Giles. 2019. "The Number and Proportion of Immigrants in the Population: International Comparisons." *Population & Societies* 563: 1–4.

Plutzer, Eric. 2002. "Becoming a Habitual Voter: Inertia, Resources, and Growth in Young Adulthood." *The American Political Science Review* 96(1): 41–56. https://doi.org/10.1017/S0003055402004227.

Porter, Ethan, and Thomas J. Wood. 2019. *False Alarm: The Truth about Political Mistruths in the Trump Era*. New York: Cambridge University Press.

Prensky, Marc. 2001. "Digital Natives, Digital Immigrants. Part 1." *On the Horizon* 9(5): 1–6.

Prior, Markus. 2010. "You've Either Got It or You Don't? The Stability of Political Interest over the Life Cycle." *The Journal of Politics* 72(3): 747–766. https://doi.org/10.1017/S0022381610000149.

Prior, Markus, Guarav Sood, and Kabir Khanna. 2015. "The Impact of Accuracy Incentives on Partisan Bias in Reports of Economic Perceptions." *Quarterly Journal of Political Science* 10: 489–518.

Putnam, Robert D. 2000. *Bowling Alone: The Collapse and Revival of American Community*. New York: Simon & Schuster.

Reef, Mary Jo, and David Knoke. 1993. "Political Alienation and Efficacy." In *Measures of Political Attitudes*, edited by John P. Robinson, Phillip R. Shaver, and Lawrence S. Wrightman, 413–464. London: Academic Press.

Reichert, Frank. 2018. "How Important Are Political Interest and Internal Political Efficacy in the Prediction of Political Participation? Longitudinal Evidence from Germany." *International Journal of Social Psychology* 33(3): 459–503. https://doi.org/10.1080/02134748.2018.1482056.

WORKS CITED 141

Reichert, Frank, and Murray Print. 2017. "Mediated and Moderated Effects of Political Communication on Civic Participation." *Information, Communication & Society* 20(8): 1162–1184. https://doi.org/10.1080/13691 18X.2016.1218524.

Reuters. 2019. "South Korea's Burned Out Millennials Choose YouTube over Samsung." March 31. https://www.reuters.com/article/us-southkorea-jobs-youtube-feature/south-koreas-burned-out-millennials-choose-youtube-over-samsung-idUSKCN1RC0YC.

Richey, Sean, and J. Benjamin Taylor. 2012. "Who Advocates? Determinants of Political Advocacy in Presidential Election Years." *Political Communication* 29(4): 414–427. https://doi.org/10.1080/10584609.2012.721869.

Riley, Matilda W. 1973. "Aging and Cohort Succession: Interpretations and Misinterpretations." *Public Opinion Quarterly* 37(1): 35–49.

Roseman, Ira J., and Craig A. Smith. 2001. "Appraisal Theory: Overview, Assumptions, Varieties, Controversies." In *Appraisal Processes in Emotion: Theory, Methods, Research*, edited by Klaus R. Scherer, Angela Schorr, and Tom Johnstone, 3–19. Series in Affective Science. New York: Oxford University Press.

Rosenstone, Steven J., and John Mark Hansen. 1993. *Mobilization, Participation, and Democracy in America*. New York: Macmillan.

Ross, Ashley D., and Stella M. Rouse. 2020. "(Young) Generations as Social Identities: The Role of Latino*Millennial/Generation Z in Shaping Attitudes about Climate Change." *Political Behavior*, online first. October 6. https://doi.org/10.1007/s11109-020-09649-8.

Rouse, Stella M., and Ashley D. Ross. 2018. *The Politics of Millennials: Political Beliefs and Policy Preferences of America's Most Diverse Generation*. Ann Arbor: University of Michigan Press.

Russo, Silvia, and Håkan Stattin. 2017. "Stability and Change in Youths' Political Interest." *Social Indicators Research* 132(2): 643–658. https://doi. org/10.1007/s11205-016-1302-9.

Sapiro, Virginia. 2004. "Not Your Parents' Political Socialization: Introduction for a New Generation." *Annual Review of Political Science* 7: 1–23.

Schlozman, Kay, Sidney Verba, and Henry E. Brady. 2012. *The Unheavenly Chorus*. Princeton, NJ: Princeton University Press.

Shames, Shauna L. 2017. *Out of the Running: Why Millennials Reject Political Careers and Why It Matters*. New York: New York University Press.

Shani, Danielle. 2009. *On the Origins of Political Interest*. Princeton: Princeton University.

Shirk, Susan, ed. 2010. *Changing Media, Changing China*. Oxford: Oxford University Press.

Sides, John, Michael Tesler, and Lynn Vavreck. 2018. *Identity Crisis: The 2016 Presidential Campaign and the Battle for the Meaning of America*. Princeton, NJ: Princeton University Press.

142 WORKS CITED

Silver, Brian D., Barbara A. Anderson, and Paul R. Abramson. 1986. "Who Overreports Voting?" *American Political Science Review* 80(2): 613–624. https://doi.org/10.2307/1958277.

Silvia, Paul J. 2006. *Exploring the Psychology of Interest*. Psychology of Human Motivation. New York: Oxford University Press.

Silvia, Paul J. 2008. "Interest—The Curious Emotion." *Current Directions in Psychological Science* 17(1): 57–60. https://doi.org/10.1111/j.1467-8721.2008.00548.x.

Smets, Kaat, and Carolien van Ham. 2013. "The Embarrassment of Riches? A Meta-Analysis of Individual-Level Research on Voter Turnout." *Electoral Studies* 32(2): 344–359. https://doi.org/10.1016/j.electstud.2012.12.006.

Somma, Nicolás M., Matías Bargsted, Rodolfo Disi Pavlic, and Rodrigo M. Medel. 2021. "No Water in the Oasis: The Chilean Spring of 2019–2020." *Social Movement Studies* 20(4): 495–502. https://doi.org/10.1080/14742 837.2020.1727737.

Strack, Fritz, and Roland Deutsch. 2004. "Reflective and Impulsive Determinants of Social Behavior." *Personality and Social Psychology Review* 8(3): 220–247. https://doi.org/10.1207/s15327957pspr0803_1.

Strömbäck, Jesper, and Adam Shehata. 2010. "Media Malaise or a Virtuous Circle? Exploring the Causal Relationships between News Media Exposure, Political News Attention and Political Interest." *European Journal of Political Research* 49(5): 575–597. https://doi.org/10.1111/j.1475-6765.2009.01913.x.

Strother, Jason. 2020. "America's BLM Protests Find Solidarity in South Korea." *The World*, June 8. https://www.pri.org/stories/2020-06-08/america-s-blm-protests-find-solidarity-south-korea.

Swire, Briony, Adam J. Berinsky, Stephan Lewandowsky, and Ullrich K. H. Ecker. 2017. "Processing Political Misinformation: Comprehending the Trump Phenomenon." *Royal Society Open Science* 4(3): 1–21.

Tajfel, Henri. 1981. *Human Groups and Social Categories*. Cambridge: Cambridge University Press.

Tajfel, Henri, and John C. Turner. 1979. "An Integrative Theory of Inter-group Conflict." In *The Social Psychology of Inter-group Relations*, edited by W. G. Austin and S. Worchel, 33–47. Monterey, CA: Brooks/Cole.

Theocharis, Yannis. 2015. "The Conceptualization of Digitally Networked Participation." *Social Media + Society* 1(2): 1–14. https://doi.org/10.1177/2056305115610140.

Theocharis, Yannis, and Jan W. van Deth. 2016. "The Continuous Expansion of Citizen Participation: A New Taxonomy." *European Political Science Review* 10(1): 139–163. https://doi.org/10.1017/S1755773916000230.

Thompson, Derek. 2012. "Adulthood, Delayed: What Has the Recession Done to Millennials?" *The Atlantic*, February 14. https://www.theatlantic.com/business/archive/2012/02/adulthood-delayed-what-has-the-recession-done-to-millennials/252913/.

WORKS CITED 143

Urban Institute. 2018. "Millennial Homeownership: Why Is It So Low, and How Can We Increase It?" https://www.urban.org/research/publication/millennial-homeownership.

Valentino, Nicholas A., Krysha Gregorowicz, and Eric W. Groenendyk. 2009. "Efficacy, Emotions and the Habit of Participation." *Political Behavior* 31(3): 307–330. https://doi.org/10.1007/s11109-008-9076-7.

Van Dam, Andrew. 2020. "The Unluckiest Generation in U.S. History." *Washington Post*, June 5. https://www.washingtonpost.com/business/2020/05/27/millennial-recession-covid/.

van Deth, Jan W. 1990. "Interest in Politics." In *Continuities in Political Action: A Longitudinal Study of Political Orientations in Three Western Democracies*, edited by M. Kent Jennings and Jan W. van Deth, 275–312. De Gruyter. https://doi.org/10.1515/9783110882193.275.

van Deth, Jan W. 2014. "A Conceptual Map of Political Participation." *Acta Politica* 49(3): 349–367. https://doi.org/10.1057/ap.2014.6.

van Deth, Jan W., and Martin Elff. 2004. "Politicisation, Economic Development and Political Interest in Europe." *European Journal of Political Research* 43(3): 477–508. https://doi.org/10.1111/j.1475-6765.2004.00162.x.

van der Linden, Sander, Edward Maibach, John Cook, Anthony Leiserowitz, and Stephan Lewandowsky. 2017. "Inoculating against Misinformation." *Science* 358(6367): 1141–1142.

van der Linden, Sander, Costas Panagopoulos, and Jon Roozenbeek. 2020. "You Are Fake News: Political Bias in Perception of Fake News." *Media, Culture & Society* 42(3): 460–470.

Van der Wal, Zeger. 2015. "'All Quiet on the Non-Western Front?' A Review of Public Service Motivation Scholarship in Non-Western Contexts." *Asia Pacific Journal of Public Administration* 37: 69–86.

Van Green, Ted, and Carroll Doherty. 2021. "Majority of U.S. Public Favors Afghanistan Troop Withdrawal; Biden Criticized for His Handling of the Situation." Pew Research Center, August 31. https://www.pewresearch.org/fact-tank/2021/08/31/majority-of-u-s-public-favors-afghanistan-troop-withdrawal-biden-criticized-for-his-handling-of-situation/.

Van Oorschot, Wim. 2006. "Making the Difference in Social Europe: Deservingness Perceptions among Citizens of European Welfare States." *Journal of European Social Policy* 16(1): 23–42.

van Zomeren, Martijn, Tamar Saguy, and Fabian M. H. Schellhaas. 2013. "Believing in "Making a Difference" to Collective Efforts: Participative Efficacy Beliefs as a Unique Predictor of Collective Action." *Group Processes & Intergroup Relations* 16(5): 618–634. https://doi.org/10.1177/136843021 2467476.

van Zomeren, Martijn, Maja Kutlaca, and Felicity Turner-Zwinkels. 2018. "Integrating Who 'We' Are with What 'We' (Will Not) Stand for: A Further Extension of the Social Identity Model of Collective Action." *European*

144 WORKS CITED

Review of Social Psychology 29(1): 122–160. https://doi.org/10.1080/10463 283.2018.1479347.

Verba, Sidney, and Norman H. Nie. 1987. *Participation in America: Political Democracy and Social Equality.* Chicago: University of Chicago Press.

Verba, Sidney, Norman H. Nie, and Jae-on Kim. 1978. *Participation and Political Equality: A Seven-Nation Comparison.* Chicago: University of Chicago Press.

Verba, Sidney, Kay Lehman Schlozman, and Henry E. Brady. 1995. *Voice and Equality: Civic Voluntarism in American Politics.* Harvard University Press.

Verba, Sidney, Kay Schlozman, and Nancy Burns. 2005. "Family Ties: Understanding the Intergenerational Transmission of Participation." In *The Social Logic of Politics,* edited by Alan Zuckerman, 94–114. Philadelphia, PA: Temple University Press.

Vertovec, Steven, and Robin Cohen. 2002. "Introduction: Conceiving Cosmopolitanism." In *Conceiving Cosmopolitanism: Theory, Context, and Practice,* edited by Steven Vertovec and Robin Cohen, 1–22. Oxford: Oxford University Press.

Vox. 2019. "'OK Boomer' Isn't Just about the Past. It's about Our Apocalyptic Future." November 19. https://www.vox.com/2019/11/19/20963757/what-is-ok-boomer-meme-about-meaning-gen-z-millennials.

Wattenberg, Martin. 2008. *Is Voting for Young People?* New York: Routledge.

Weinmann, Carina. 2017. "Feeling Political Interest while Being Entertained? Explaining The Emotional Experience of Interest in Politics in the Context of Political Entertainment Programs." *Psychology of Popular Media Culture* 6(2): 123–141. https://doi.org/10.1037/ppm0000091.

Whiteley, Paul F. 2011. "Is the Party over? The Decline of Party Activism and Membership across the Democratic World." *Party Politics* 17(1): 21–44. https://doi.org/10.1177/1354068810365505.

World Economic Forum. 2016. "Millennials Will Be the First Generation to Earn Less Than Their Parents." July 19. https://www.weforum.org/agenda/2016/07/millennials-will-be-the-first-generation-to-earn-less-than-their-parents/.

World Economic Forum. 2019. "This Graph Tells Us Who's Using Social Media the Most." October 2. https://www.weforum.org/agenda/2019/10/social-media-use-by-generation/.

World Economic Forum. 2021. "There Are 1.8 Billion Millennials on Earth. Here's Where They Live." November 8. https://www.weforum.org/agenda/2021/11/millennials-world-regional-breakdown/#:~:text=A%20r egional%20breakdown%20of%20millennials%20around%20the%20wo rld&text=Millennials%2C%20defined%20as%20those%20born,the%20 largest%20adult%20cohort%20worldwide.

Wright, James D. 1981. "Political Disaffection." In *The Handbook of Political Behavior: Volume 4,* edited by Samuel L. Long, 1–79. New York: Springer. https://doi.org/10.1007/978-1-4684-3878-9_1.

WORKS CITED   145

Yeager, David S., Samuel B. Larson, Jon A. Krosnick, and Trevor Tompson. 2011. "Measuring Americans' Issue Priorities: A New Version of the Most Important Problem Question Reveals More Concern about Global Warming and the Environment." *Public Opinion Quarterly* 75(1): 125–138.

Zachara, Małgorzata. 2020. "To Vote or Not to Vote? The Political Orientations of Millennials in a Comparative Perspective." *Society and Economy* 42(3): 229–244. https://doi.org/10.1556/204.2020.00016.

Zerba, Amy. 2011. "Young Adults' Reasons behind Avoidances of Daily Print Newspapers and Their Ideas for Change." *Journalism & Mass Communication Quarterly* 88(3): 597–614.

Zhuravskaya, Ekaterina, Maria Petrova, and Ruben Enikolopov. 2020. "Political Effects of the Internet and Social Media." *Annual Review of Economics* 12: 415–438.

Zogby, John, and Joan Snyder Kuhl. 2013. *First Globals: Understanding, Managing, and Unleashing the Potential of Our Millennial Generation.* New York: John Zogby.

Index

For the benefit of digital users, indexed terms that span two pages (e.g., 52–53) may, on occasion, appear on only one of those pages.
Figures are indicated by *f* following the page number

activism. *See* political activism
Afghanistan, withdrawal of United States from, 117
Antunovic, Dunja, 42
Arab Spring, 7, 17
Australia
  "citizen of the world" label and, 28
  contacting politicians in, 71
  eschewing of labels in, 21–22
  gender identity in, 35–36
  government spending support in, 56–58
  national identity in, 22–28, 106
  political activity in, 83–84, 87–88, 114
  political donations in, 71
  political organizations in, 84, 97, 114, 116
  public service leadership in, 116–17
  religious identity in, 31
  sources of political information in, 45–47
  volunteerism in, 115–16
  voter turnout in, 68–69

Baby Boomers, social media use by, 16–17
Bartels, Larry M., 17–18
belonging, sense of, 90–91
Biden, Joe, 117–18

Black Lives Matter movement, 102
boycotts, 82–83
Braungart, Margaret M., 2
Braungart, Richard, 2

Chile
  "citizen of the world" label and, 28
  eschewing of labels in, 21–22
  gender identity in, 35–36
  government spending support in, 56–58
  national identity in, 22–28, 106
  petition signing in, 69
  political activity in, 83–84, 95–96
  political efficacy in, 81–82, 87–88, 113–14
  political internet forums in, 71–73
  political organizations in, 84
  public service leadership in, 116–17
  religious identity in, 30–31
  social networks for political activities in, 113
  sources of political information in, 45
  volunteerism in, 115–16
  voter turnout in, 68–69
citizen engagement, political interest and, 77
"citizen of the world"
  as age effect, 37–38

148   INDEX

"citizen of the world" (*cont.*)
  climate change and, 117–18
  importance of identity, 25*f*, 28–29
  nationalism *vs.*, 13–14, 18, 20,
    36–37, 106
  "new media" and, 101,
    108, 110–11
  problem-solving and, 118
  strength of identity, 14–15, 20–
    21, 23*f*
civic participation as political
    participation, 65
class identity, 20–21, 23*f*, 25*f*, 34–
    35, 107–8
"clickbait," 43
climate crisis, 117–18
Cooke, Tanner R., 42
"core personas," 2–3
cosmopolitanism. *See* "citizen of
    the world"
COVID-19 pandemic, 2–3, 104–5

Dalton, Russell J., 82–83
democracy
  challenges to, 77–78
  political efficacy and, 79–81
  political engagement and, 64, 87–
    88, 89, 99
demonstrations, 17, 69–71, 70*f*, 82–
    83, 90, 112–13
"digital immigrants," 103
"digital natives," 39, 101
diplomacy, support for, 56, 58–59,
    60*f*, 61
disinformation, political, 43, 48–49,
    62–63. *See also* misinformation,
    political
diversity, demographic, 16–17, 28–
    29, 105
donations, political, 71, 74*f*, 86–
    87, 90
Dutch Reformed Church, 32

"duty-based citizenship"
  decline in, 64–65
  generational difference and, 66,
    67–68, 82–83, 111–12, 114–15
  See also organizations, political;
    volunteerism; voting

economic environment, attitudinal
    change and, 4
education levels, 4, 28–29
employees, loyalty of, 5
"engaged citizenship," 69–73
  generational difference and, 66,
    82–83, 86–87, 95–96, 111–
    13, 114–15
  increase in, 64–65, 90
  local politics and, 96–97, 116
  See also demonstrations;
    donations, political; internet
    forums, political; petition
    signing; protest movements
ethnic identity, 20–21, 23*f*, 25*f*,
    34, 107–8
European Social Survey, 77–78

Facebook, 17, 39, 42
"fake news," 49–50
Floyd, George, 102
foreign policy, 109–11. *See also*
    diplomacy, support for
formal behavioral measures, 73. *See
    also* "duty-based citizenship"

Gallup, 5, 91
gender identity, 20–21, 23*f*, 25*f*, 34–
    36, 107–8
generational effects, 7–8, 37–38
"generational frame," 2
generational identity
  importance of, 25*f*
  of Millennials, 29–30, 61–62, 103–
    4, 105–8, 117–18

INDEX 149

strength of, 23*f*
Generation Z, 39
German Longitudinal Election
    Study, 81
global citizenship. *See* "citizen of
    the world"
globalization, 12–13, 16–17, 28–29
Global Millennial Survey (GMS),
    6–7, 18–19, 34–36, 119–27
Global Web Index, 16–17
government spending, support for,
    56–58, 57*f*, 59–60, 63, 109–11
Great Recession, 104–5

healthcare, government involvement
    in, 56, 58*f*, 58, 59*f*, 60–61,
    63, 109–11
Hong Kong, 17
"How Millennials Want to Work and
    Live" (Gallup), 91

idealism, 37–38
identities
    importance of, 18–22
    mean ratings of, 21*f*
    takeaways from the GMS, 34–36
    See also class identity; ethnic
        identity; gender identity;
        generational identity; national
        identity; religious identity;
        social identity
"identity publics," 33, 35–36, 107–8
information choice, 41–42
Instagram, 17, 39
interconnectedness, digital, 2–
    3, 28–29
interconnectedness, global, 12–
    13, 16–17
internet
    difficulty determining accuracy
        of political information from,
        52*f*, 53*f*

"digital natives" and, 39
interconnectedness and, 2–
    3, 28–29
policy preferences and, 59,
    61, 110–11
political interest and, 53–54
as source of political information,
    45, 46*f*, 47–48, 62, 108
internet forums, political, 71–73,
    86–87, 90
"issue publics," 35–36

Jackman, Simon, 17–18
Jardina, Ashley, 19–20
journalism, shift in, 39

Kim, Sangmook, 65–66

labels, eschewing of
    "citizen of the world" and, 14–15,
        18, 20–22, 28–29, 36–37
    generational identity and, 29, 30
    race/gender and, 35
leadership gap, 91, 97–98, 99–
    100, 116–17
lifestyle patterns, political
    engagement and, 90–91, 99–
    100, 115

meetings, political. *See* rallies,
    political
Mexico
    acceptance of labels in, 20–21
    class identity in, 34
    ethnic identity in, 34
    political activism in, 73–75, 83–
        84, 86–87
    political donations in, 71
    political efficacy in, 81–82
    political interest in, 78
    political internet forums in, 71–73
    political organizations in, 84, 97

150 INDEX

Mexico (*cont.*)
  political rallies in, 71
  public service leadership
    in, 116–17
  religious identity in, 31
  social networks for political
    activities in, 113
  volunteerism in, 115–16
  voter turnout in, 73–75
Millennial Generation
  characterizations of, 102–3
  defined, 1, 11–12
  generational identity of, 7–8, 12,
    14–15, 29–30, 61–62, 103–
    4, 117–18
  as global citizens, 117–18
misinformation, political, 43–44
  difficulty determining, 48–52, 52*f*,
    53*f*, 56, 108–9
  low political interest and, 54–55
  social media and, 43
  See also political information
mobility, geographic, 90–91
multiculturalism, 13–14

national identity, 22–29, 36–37, 106
  vs. "citizen of the world," 37
  importance of, 13–14, 25*f*, 36–37
  strength of, 14–15, 23*f*, 106
"new media"
  difficulty determining accuracy of
    political information on, 50–52,
    52*f*, 53*f*, 62–63
  policy preferences and, 61
  as source of political information,
    40–41, 47–48, 48*f*, 62, 108
  See also internet; social media
news consumption as polarized, 42
news industry, 39
newspapers
  difficulty determining accuracy of
    political information from, 51–52

  as source of political information,
    46*f*, 47
news sources, online
  generational use of, 48*f*
  incidental exposure to, 41
  paid subscriptions to, 43
  potential for bias in, 42
New Zealand
  "citizen of the world" and, 28
  contacting politicians in, 71
  gender identity in, 35–36
  generational identity in, 29, 107
  government spending support
    in, 56–58
  national identity in, 22–28, 106
  political activity in, 83–84, 87–
    88, 114
  political internet forums in, 71–73
  political organizations in, 84, 97,
    114, 116
  public service leadership
    in, 116–17
  racial identity in, 33–34
  religious identity in, 30–31
  social networks for political
    activities in, 113
  sources of political
    information in, 47
  voter turnout in, 68–69
Nie, Norman H., 65–66
Nussbaum, Martha C., 37

Obama, Barack, 18
Occupy Wall Street, 17
"OK Boomer," 17
online news. *See* news
  sources, online
organizations, political
  importance of joining, 84, 85*f*, 88
  local, 90, 96*f*, 96–97, 115–17
  national, 114
Oxford, University of, 43

Paris Agreement, 117–18
Parsons, Patrick, 42
patriotism. *See* national identity
peer networks, political socialization and, 16–17
Perry, James L., 91–92
petition signing, 67, 69, 70*f*, 73, 112
Pew Research Center, 4, 29–30
police brutality, 17
political activism
  behavioral measures, 73
  "engaged citizenship" and, 76*f*
  generational differences in, 66, 73–75, 88, 114
  importance of, 85*f*
  local level, 95*f*, 95–96
  voting and, 88
political behaviors, importance of, 75
political campaigns, 65
political content on social media, 42
political discussion as polarized, 42
political efficacy, 79–82, 80*f*, 113–14
"political generations," 2
political information
  ability to find, 40–41
  accuracy of, 48–52, 50*f*, 51*f*, 52*f*, 108–9
  internet as source of, 53–54
  "new media" as source of, 40–41, 45, 108
  public policy preferences and, 59–61, 61*f*, 110–11
  social media as, 40
  sources of, 44–48
  See also "new media"; newspapers; news sources, online; radio, political information via; television
political interest, 54*f*, 80*f*
  across generations, 41, 63, 87–88, 109, 113
  appraisal theories of emotions and, 75–77

citizen engagement and, 77
lack of as challenge to democracy, 77–78
in local issues, 92
misinformation campaigns and, 54–55
news sources and, 52–56, 55*f*
political participation and, 75–78, 81
social media and increase in, 41–42
political opinions, "new media" and, 39
political organizations. *See* organizations, political
political participation, 64–67
  decrease in, 65
  defined, 65–66
  "duty-based" *vs.* "engaged," 64–66, 67–73, 81, 86–87, 111–12
  importance of different forms of, 82–84
  indicators of, 73–75
  political efficacy and, 79–82
  as stable, 77–78
  See also "duty-based citizenship"; "engaged citizenship"
political socialization, 15–18
politicians, contacting, 65, 71, 72*f*, 112
poverty rates, 2–3, 4
Prior, Markus, 77–78
protest movements, 17, 65, 69–71, 102, 112–13
public policy preferences, 56–62, 61*f*, 109–11
public service leadership, 90, 97–99, 98*f*, 115, 116–17
"public service motivation," 91–92

racial identity, 19–20, 23*f*, 25*f*, 33–35, 107–8
racial justice, 102

152 INDEX

radio, political information via, 46*f*, 47, 51–52
rallies, political, 71, 72*f*, 112
Reichert, Frank, 81
religious identity, 14–15, 23*f*, 25*f*, 30–33, 107–8
Reuters Institute, 43
role models, political, 18
Ross, Ashley D., 103
Rouse, Stella M., 103
Russo, Silvia, 77–78

September 11, 2001, 17–18, 103
Shani, Danielle, 77–78
Shim Ji-hoon, 102
Silent Generation, 2
Silvia, Paul J., 75–77
smartphones, interconnectedness and, 2–3, 28–29
social activities as political participation, 65
social change, 13–14
social identity, 18–19
social media
    accuracy of political information from, 52*f*, 53*f*
    "digital natives" and, 39
    incidental exposure to news through, 42
    misinformation campaigns and, 43, 54–55
    policy preferences and, 59–61, 110–11
    political interest and, 41–42, 54–55, 109
    as political organizing tool, 17, 71–73, 113
    as source of political information, 40, 45, 46*f*, 47–48, 62, 108
    use of, 16–17
social networks
    political activities and, 65

political socialization and, 16–17
South Africa
    government healthcare support in, 58
    government spending support in, 56–58
    importance of political activism in, 83–84
    internet as source of political information in, 45
    national identity in, 22, 27–28, 106
    political donations in, 71
    political efficacy in, 81–82
    political internet forums in, 71–73
    political organizations in, 84, 97
    political rallies in, 71
    public service leadership in, 116–17
    religious identity in, 30–33, 107–8
    social networks for political activities in, 113
    volunteerism in, 115–16
    voter turnout in, 68–69
South Korea
    accuracy of political information in, 49–50, 108–9
    class identity in, 34, 35–36
    eschewing of labels in, 21–22
    generational identity in, 29–30, 107
    government healthcare support in, 58
    government spending support in, 56–58
    importance of political activism in, 83–84
    internet as top source of political information in, 45
    national identity in, 22–27, 106
    petition signing in, 69
    political organizations in, 84, 95–96, 97

INDEX   153

public service leadership
in, 116–17
racial justice protests in, 102
religious identity in, 31
voter turnout in, 68–69, 73–75,
86, 112
Stattin, Håkan, 77–78
"Stop Kony" campaign, 17
student debt, 4

technology
Millennial identity and, 39, 102–3
political socialization and, 16–17
television
accuracy of political information
from, 51–52
policy preferences and, 59–
61, 110–11
political interest and, 55–56
as source of political news, 45–47,
46f, 55–56
Thunberg, Greta, 18
Trump, Donald, 19–20, 117–18
Tutu, Desmond, 32
Twitter, 17, 39, 42

unemployment, 2–3, 29–30
United Kingdom
gender identity in, 35–36
generational identity in, 29, 107
political activity in, 83–84, 87–
88, 114
political organizations in, 84, 97,
114, 116
public service leadership
in, 116–17
religious identity in, 30–31
sources of political information
in, 45–47
voter turnout in, 68–69
United Nations Climate Change
Conference (COP26), 117–18

United States
accuracy of political information
in, 49–50, 108–9
"citizen of the world" and, 28
contacting politicians in, 71
diplomacy support in, 58–59, 111
eschewing of labels in, 21–22
generational identity in, 29, 107
government healthcare
support in, 58
importance of political activism
in, 83–84
national identity in, 22–28, 106
political efficacy in, 81–82
political interest in, 77–78, 87–88
political organizations in, 84
political rallies in, 71
public service leadership in, 97–
98, 116–17
racial identity in, 33–34
religious identity in, 30–31, 32–
33, 107–8
sources of political information
in, 45–47
volunteerism in, 115–16
white identity in, 19–20
withdrawal from Afghanistan, 117
universalism. *See* "citizen of
the world"

Valentino, Nicholas A., 79–81
Van Deth, Jan W., 65–66
Verba, Sidney, 65–66
Vietnam War, 17–18
volunteerism, 82–83, 90, 93–95,
94f, 115–16
voting
activism and, 65, 88
activist indicators and, 73–75
decrease in, 64–65, 66, 89–90
"duty-based citizenship"
and, 82–83

154 INDEX

voting (*cont.*)
    importance of, 83, 85*f*, 86, 114
    in local elections, 92–93,
        93*f*, 115–16
    political interest and, 77, 94–95
    turnout, 67–69, 68*f*, 112

"war on terror," 17–18, 103
Watergate break-in, 17–18
white identity, 19–20

Wise, Lois Recascino, 91–92
women in public office, 97–98
workforce behaviors, political
    engagement and, 99–100

X González, 18

Yousafzai, Malala, 18
Youth-Parent Socialization Study,
    77–78

Printed in the USA/Agawam, MA
November 16, 2022

801347.011